Disclaimer

The publisher of this book is by no way associated with the National Institute of Standards and Technology (NIST). The NIST did not publish this book. It was published by 50 page publications under the public domain license.

50 Page Publications.

Book Title: EEEL - Office of Law Enforcement Standards - Programs, Activities, and Accomplishments

Book Author: Thomas J. Russell

Book Abstract: The Office of Law Enforcement Standards (OLES) at the National Institute of Standards and Technology (NIST)helps law enforcement and criminal justice agencies ensure that the equipment they purchase and the technologies that use are safe, dependable, and highly effective. This publication summarizes the FY-06 accomplishments and the FY-07 programs and goals.

Citation: NIST Interagency/Internal Report (NISTIR) - IR 7366

Keyword: accomplishments;goals;objectives;OLES;programs;staff

January 2007

For additional information contact:
Telephone: (301) 975-2757
Facsimile: (301) 948-0978
On the Web: http://www.eeel.nist.gov/oles/

THE ELECTRONICS AND ELECTRICAL ENGINEERING LABORATORY

One of NIST's seven Measurement and Standards Laboratories, EEEL conducts research, provides measurement services, and helps set standards in support of: the fundamental electronic technologies of semiconductors, magnetics, and superconductors; information and communications technologies, such as fiber optics, photonics, microwaves, electronic displays, and electronics manufacturing supply chain collaboration; forensics and security measurement instrumentation; fundamental and practical physical standards and measurement services for electrical quantities; maintaining the quality and integrity of electrical power systems; and the development of nanoscale and microelectromechanical devices. EEEL provides support to law enforcement, corrections, and criminal justice agencies, including homeland security.

EEEL consists of four programmatic divisions and two matrix-managed offices:

Semiconductor Electronics Division

Optoelectronics Division

Quantum Electrical Metrology Division

Electromagnetics Division

Office of Microelectronics Programs

Office of Law Enforcement Standards

This document describes the technical programs of the Office of Law Enforcement Standards (OLES). Similar documents describing the other Divisions and Offices are available. Contact NIST/EEEL, 100 Bureau Drive, MS 8100, Gaithersburg, MD 20899-8100, Telephone: (301) 975-2220, On the Web: www.eeel.nist.gov

Cover caption: The Office of Law Enforcement Standards (OLES) helps criminal justice, public safety, emergency responder, and homeland security agencies make informed procurement, deployment, applications, operating, and training decisions primarily by developing performance standards, measurement tools, operating procedures, and equipment guidelines. Our logo (top center) reflects some of the projects that we conduct: DNA research, arson research, forensic sciences, and law enforcement weapons and equipment. Shown on the cover are pictures that represent some of the projects in our portfolio: development of standards for ballistic resistance of personal body armor, bomb disposal robot standards, and computer forensic reference data sets.

ELECTRONICS AND ELECTRICAL ENGINEERING LABORATORY

OFFICE OF LAW ENFORCEMENT STANDARDS

PROGRAMS, ACTIVITIES, AND ACCOMPLISHMENTS

NISTIR 7366

January 2007

U.S. DEPARTMENT OF COMMERCE
Carlos M. Gutierrez, Secretary

Technology Administration
Robert Cresanti, Under Secretary of Commerce for Technology

National Institute of Standards and Technology
William Jeffrey, Director

Any mention of commercial products is for information only; it does not imply recommendation or endorsement by the National Institute of Standards and Technology nor does it imply that the products mentioned are necessarily the best available for the purpose.

Contents

Welcome v

Mission v

Organization vi

    Developing Performance Standards vi

Office of Law Enforcement Standards Staff (810.02) vii

Weapons and Protective Systems 1

  Body Armor Program...1

    Project: Testing of ZYLON®-Based Body Armor 1

    Project: Development of Methodologies for Service Life Prediction and Accelerated Testing of Soft Body Armor 4

    Project: Correlation of Fiber Properties to Ballistic Resistance.......................................6

    Project: Ballistic Limit Evaluation 9

    Project: Conformity Assessment Program Development 9

    Project: Development and Validation of Short-Term Artificial Aging Protocol for Soft Body Armor 10

    Project: Review and Update of the Ballistic-Resistant Body Armor Standard 11

    Project: Blunt Trauma Research and Development of an Improved Test Methodology..12

    Project: Bullet Deformation Behavior 13

    Protective Equipment Program 14

    Project: NIJ Standard–0106.01, "Ballistic Helmets" 14

    Project: NIJ Standard–0108.01, "Ballistic Resistance of Protective Materials" 15

    Project: NIJ Standard–0104.02, "Riot Helmets and Face Shields" 15

Detection, Inspection, and Enforcement Technologies 17

    Project: NIJ Standard–0601.02, "Walk-Through Metal Detectors for Use in Concealed Weapon and Contraband Detection" 18

    Project: NIJ Standard–0602.02, "Handheld Metal Detectors for Use in Concealed Weapon and Contraband Detection" 19

    Project: Evaluation of Biometric Recognition Systems 19

    Project: Fast Capture Evaluation 20

  Project: Technologies for Traffic Enforcement 21

    Project: Imaging Metrology 21

    Project: Through-Wall Imaging and Surveillance 23

    Project: Concealed Weapon Detection and Imaging 24

Forensic Sciences 26

    Project: Computer Forensic Reference Data Sets (CFReDS) 26

    Project: Computer Forensics Tools Testing (CFTT) 26

- Project: DNA Related Projects 27
- Project: Ion Mobility Spectrometry (IMS) Trace Drug Detection Devices 27
- Project: National Software Reference Library (NSRL) 28
- Project: Standard Casing Reference Material 29
- Project: Real Time Forensics Imaging for Analog and Digital Video Tapes 29
- Project: Refractive Index Glass Standard Reference Material 30

Public Safety Communication Systems 33
- Project: Standardization Efforts Related to Telecommunication and Information Technology Interoperability 33

CBRNE Standards 38
- Shared Management Responsibilities 38
- Meeting Customer Requirements 38
- Project Funding and Execution 38
- Critical Incident Technologies (CIT) 40
- Public Safety and Security Technologies 44

WELCOME

The Office of Law Enforcement Standards (OLES) helps criminal justice, public safety, emergency responder, and homeland security agencies make informed procurement, deployment, applications, operating, and training decisions, primarily by developing performance standards, measurement tools, operating procedures and equipment guidelines. OLES is part of the Electronics and Electrical Engineering Laboratory (EEEL) of the National Institute of Standards and Technology (NIST). OLES, with a staff of 18, is located on the NIST campus in Gaithersburg, Maryland.

MISSION

Unique among NIST's program offices, the Office of Law Enforcement Standards (OLES) addresses the technology and metrology needs of the criminal justice, public safety, public security and greater homeland security communities. For 35 years, OLES's customers have been corrections personnel, forensic scientists and those who are today known as "first responders" – police officers, firefighters, and others responsible for the safety and security of people and property. Through our work on performance standards for critical technologies such as ballistic body armor, metal detectors, chemical systems and protective equipment, computer forensics, DNA analysis, and public safety communications, OLES has developed unique expertise. And through our working relationships with criminal justice, public safety and public security practitioners, universities, government agencies, professional and scientific organizations, and offices and laboratories throughout NIST, OLES has developed a vast network of resources that can be brought to bear on solving difficult technical challenges.

In 1999 that expertise and those resources earned OLES an invitation to serve on the Standards Coordination Committee of the newly formed InterAgency Board for Equipment Standardization and Interoperability (IAB). Immediately, IAB asked OLES to address one of its highest priorities: developing requirement standards for respiratory protection equipment to ensure that emergency responders would survive chemical warfare agent attacks. This firsthand experience at tackling the challenges of CBRNE countermeasures prepared OLES for the roles it fulfills today. Following the events of September 11, 2001, OLES found itself leading several technical programs related to homeland security. OLES personnel have assumed key roles as managers and consultants at the Department of Homeland Security. OLES has led the efforts of NIST's Homeland Security Strategic Working Group. And, perhaps, most indicative of OLES's reputation and competence, the Office's operating budget, derived entirely from work with agencies outside NIST, grew from about $900,000 in FY1996 to more than $50 million in FY2006.

In addition to developing minimum performance standards, OLES develops reference materials (RMs) and standard reference materials (SRMs) for use in test procedures and to calibrate equipment. OLES develops technology and metrology to support the advancement of equipment and methods used to address the needs of criminal justice, public safety, emergency responder and homeland security agencies. OLES authors equipment user guides; designs methods for examining evidentiary materials; develops technology where appropriate and applicable; and provides technical advice and assistance to agencies throughout the criminal justice, public safety, emergency responder and homeland security communities. OLES staff members hold memberships in scores of technical and scientific organizations, chair technical and policy-making committees in several of those organizations, and work closely with technical experts throughout the public and private sectors.

ORGANIZATION

OLES is a program management organization that designs and manages standards-development and research projects on behalf of agencies such as the Department of Homeland Security (DHS), the National Institute of Justice (NIJ), and others. OLES also maintains metrology activities and laboratories for equipment unique to law enforcement and criminal justice agents and emergency responders.

Within OLES are six program areas: Weapons and Protective Systems; Detection, Inspection, and Enforcement Technologies; Forensic Sciences; Public Safety Communication Systems; and Critical Incident Technologies; and Public Safety and Security Technologies. These program areas conduct a vast range of projects related to protective clothing, communication systems, investigative aids, security devices, traffic enforcement equipment, vehicles, firearms and ammunition, detection of concealed weapons and explosives, forensic science, homeland security, and domestic preparedness.

Proposed and continuing projects within each program area for FY2007 are described in this publication.

DEVELOPING PERFORMANCE STANDARDS

Developing performance standards is OLES' primary activity, and the process OLES follows in that work provides a good illustration of the organization and its function.

Developing a performance standard begins when the criminal justice, public safety, emergency responder and/or homeland security community identifies the need for a certain type of equipment to perform at a certain level in the field. A bullet-resistant vest must stop a new type of ammunition. A metal detector must be sensitive enough for thorough screening of airline passengers. A respirator must allow first responders to work safely in a chemical, biological or radiological hot zone.

OLES talks to equipment users to refine our understanding of how the equipment is employed and under what conditions. OLES designs research projects to gather information from manufacturers and technical experts, and to evaluate the capabilities of equipment available on the market. OLES formulates a set of performance criteria that the particular type of equipment must meet to be considered adequate. Then OLES devises tests that can be used to determine if a piece of equipment meets the criteria. Together, the performance criteria and the test methods make up what is called a minimum performance standard.

The draft minimum performance standard is reviewed and commented on by practitioners, manufacturers, technical experts, government agencies and other parties with a professional interest in the standard. After required revisions, the minimum performance standard is published and distributed, along with a report that provides manufacturers and designers with detailed technical information about the standard, and a user guide to help agencies and their personnel understand the standard and properly select, use and maintain the equipment.

For additional information about OLES, please visit us at http://www.eeel.nist.gov/oles.

OFFICE OF LAW ENFORCEMENT STANDARDS STAFF (810.02)

Staff may be contacted at the following telephone extensions (301–975–XXXX) or by email at firstname.lastname@nist.gov.

Name	Title	Extension
Kathleen Higgins	Director, OLES	2754
Thomas Russell	Special Assistant to the Director	2665
Sharon Ellison	Administrative Support Assistant	2757
Melissa Naddeo	Office Manager	2756
Susan Ballou	Program Manager: Forensic Sciences	8750
Brian Briggman	Contractor: Information Technology Specialist	8009
Alim Fatah	Program Manager: Public Safety and Security Technologies	2753
Amanda Forster	Materials Research Engineer: Weapons and Protective Systems	5632
Pamela Gray	Contractor: Critical Incident Technologies	4511
Donald Larson	Electronics Engineer: Detection, Inspection, and Enforcement Technologies	3183
Philip Mattson	Program Manager: Critical Incident Technologies	3396
Dereck Orr	Program Manager: Public Safety Communication Systems	2296
Nicholas Paulter	Program Manager: Detection, Inspection, and Enforcement Technologies	2405
Kirk Rice	Program Manager: Weapons and Protective Systems	8071
Michael Riley	Program Manager: Weapons and Protective Systems – Research, Test, and Evaluation	6065
Lisa Rothwell	Contractor: Public Safety and Security Technologies	8021
James Stewart	Contractor: Critical Incident Technologies	2352
Nathaniel Waters	Engineering Technician	5128

Weapons and Protective Systems

OLES' Weapons and Protective Systems program provides ongoing technical support and research for the National Institute of Justice (NIJ) standard for ballistic-resistant body armor (bullet-resistant vests), which OLES first developed for NIJ in 1972. The body armor program is part of NIJ's successful Law Enforcement and Corrections Standards and Testing Program, through which companies may have their products voluntarily certified as compliant with the standard. Ballistic-resistant body armor has been credited with saving more than 3000 lives, and the program's evaluations of new materials and ballistic threats and its revisions of the standard help ensure the continued effectiveness of this technology. The Weapons and Protective Systems program also develops and supports other equipment performance standards vital to the safety of law enforcement and corrections personnel, including stab-resistant body armor; ballistic helmets; riot helmets and face shields; metallic handcuffs; and firearms.

In recent years, the Weapons and Protective Systems program area has focused heavily on the ballistic-resistant body armor program, providing standards development services and technical support to the compliance testing program, conducting and overseeing research leading to improvements in the standards, participating in technical and practitioner communities, establishing collaborations with other contributors, addressing emerging armor issues, and recommending improvements to the standards and associated certification programs.

Body Armor Program

The NIJ body armor program consists of two basic components: a standards development program, and a compliance testing program that uses the current version of the body armor standard, NIJ Standard–0101.04. The NIJ body armor program provides law enforcement officers and public safety officials with an independent assessment that the armor they wear provides a reasonable level of ballistic protection. This program is critical because the public safety community depends upon objective third-party testing, such as that provided through the NIJ testing program, to assist them in making informed purchasing decisions about important life safety equipment.

To ensure that the program remains valuable and has broad appeal, NIJ bears the responsibility to monitor developments in the industry and the field, and to gather feedback from practitioners and other users of the standard. The former provides knowledge about new and improving ballistic-resistant materials, changing ballistic threats, and the introduction of special types of body armor; while the latter provides insight into what users expect of body armor, and any special considerations that should be addressed because of the way body armor is used or tested. Through these efforts, numerous issues have been identified over a number of years, and these generally have formed the basis for research or administrative initiatives aimed at further enhancements to the standard or the compliance testing program.

There are a number of projects included under this program. Generally they are focused on critically examining the performance of ballistic materials in the field to forewarn of any potential problems that may be developing, improving our understanding of body armor performance, increasing the quality demands placed upon armor manufacturers, and refining test body armor test methodologies.

Project: Testing of ZYLON®-Based Body Armor

Goals

To conduct a comprehensive testing program to address concerns with the ongoing ballistic-resistant performance of ZYLON-based body armor in response to the Department of Justice's Body Armor Safety Initiative, announced by Attorney General Ashcroft on November 18, 2003. This initiative came in response to concerns raised by the public safety community and members of Congress regarding the performance of ZYLON-based armor. ZYLON is the trade name for a high strength ballistic fiber known as poly (p-phenylenebenzoxazole) (PBO).

Customer Needs

Neither the NIJ Standard–0101.04, "Ballistic Resistance of Personal Body Armor," nor the current Body Armor Compliance Testing Program were originally intended to address the ongoing performance of used ballistic-resistant body armor. Ensuring ongoing ballistic-resistant performance has always been the responsibility of the body armor manufacturer. The ZYLON-based body armor concern has heightened an industry-wide awareness that ongoing ballistic performance must be satisfactorily addressed. Determinations and

Technical Contacts:
Kirk Rice
Amanda Forster
Michael Riley
Nathaniel Waters

Staff-Years:
12

findings of this testing program are expected to highlight significant problems with some samples of body armor, lead to improved body armor performance standards, and very likely produce fundamental changes in the Compliance Testing Program, ultimately benefiting the users of body armor. The primary benefit anticipated will be the implementation of ongoing conformity assessment methods that will give criminal justice and public safety officers greater confidence in the performance of body armor.

Technical Strategy

The Body Armor Safety Initiative directs NIJ to conduct an immediate review of both new and used ZYLON-based bullet resistant vests to ensure that they are effective, and to include in this testing effort the upgrade kits provided by manufacturers to retrofit ZYLON-based armor. To address the requirements, multiple test efforts comprise this project: 1) Forest Hills Vest Study, 2) ZYLON-containing body armor Ballistic Performance Tests, and 3) Upgrade Kit Tests. Over the past two years, these projects have been described in prior program plans, details of the testing activities were presented in separate documents, and results of those activities were published in three reports to the Attorney General and several other technical reports. These activities also developed information that led to NIJ's establishment of the 2005 Interim Requirements. A brief summary of the status of each study follows:

Forest Hills Vest Penetration Study

The Forest Hills vest penetration has been described as the first known instance in which an NIJ-compliant armor model appears to have failed to stop a bullet that it was designed to defeat. Because the Forest Hills vest had been in service for only six months prior to the incident, it was originally believed that the officer's vest would be nearly identical to a newly constructed vest. Upon discovering that the mechanical properties of the ZYLON yarns from the Forest Hills vest were diminished, and that those changes were likely due to chemical degradation, the Forest Hills tests focused on studying the five factors that were considered the most likely to have contributed to degradation.

Since the ZYLON in the Forest Hills vest was found to be much weaker than expected, it became necessary to test armor that had been weakened to a condition matching that of the penetrated vest. For these studies to be successful, they are predicated on establishing an equivalency between artificially degraded armor panels and the officer's body armor. This was attempted through chemical degradation by developing an aging process relying on hydrolytic (moisture-induced) degradation to achieve uniform degradation of the ballistic materials. This aging involves holding the test specimens at elevated conditions of temperature and humidity, and periodically subjecting extracted yarns to quasi-static tensile tests until the degraded mechanical properties were obtained.

The studies originally planned were completed and reported on in status reports to the Attorney General. While these earlier studies contributed a great deal of understanding to the factors that influence ballistic degradation of ZYLON-based body armor, no combination of factors produced a penetration that would fully explain the failure of the Forest Hills body armor. This possibility was considered during the original planning, and additional armor test specimens were set aside to support future work.

Recognized then were several other factors that could be important, but also difficult to quantify, such as the effects mechanical damage might have on mechanical and ballistic performance, or the differences between quasi-static and high-rate mechanical properties. Follow-on vest studies were postponed until more advances could be made in this area. Research continued last year to develop controlled mechanical exposure tests of ZYLON and to examine the differences between quasi-static and dynamic properties of ballistic materials. An additional ballistic penetration test series is planned using the body armor panels that were set aside from the original study. Details regarding how to achieve controlled mechanical exposures and how to measure mechanically-induced changes are part of the Artificial Aging project described elsewhere, and this test effort will be tied into that other effort.

DELIVERABLES

- Test plan for mechanical exposure of remaining Forest Hills armor panels, assessing changes in the armor panels, and ballistic testing of the armor panels.

- Report on high-rate mechanical properties of ZYLON.

BALLISTIC PERFORMANCE TESTS OF ZYLON-CONTAINING BODY ARMOR

There were more than 240 different models of ZYLON-based ballistic-resistant body resistant body armor from 16 different manufacturers that had been found to comply with either NIJ Standard–0101.04 or NIJ Standard–0101.03, "Ballistic Resistance of Police Body Armor." It is estimated that there are/were at least 300,000 ZYLON-based armors in field use. Drawing valid conclusions about all ZYLON-based armor performance requires a significant testing effort. A two-phase test plan was developed to provide an early indication of whether there were ballistic performance concerns and to help ensure that a representative sampling of used armors (e.g. different manufacturers, threat levels, designs, environmental conditions, age, etc.) would be tested. A brief summary of these phases follows.

PHASE I – "WORST CASE TESTING"

A set of abbreviated ballistic tests (V50 and penetration) were conducted on a limited number of used ZYLON armors that were moderately to heavily worn. All body armor samples were donated to the testing program by law enforcement agencies. The front panel of each vest was subjected to normal ballistic penetration testing. The original compliance testing would have required six shots of one caliber (bullet type) on a ballistic armor panel, and a different ballistic armor panel would have received six shots of a second caliber. This testing required the same two threat rounds, except both were fired into the same armor panel; three shots of one caliber and three shots of the other. Furthermore, backface signature measurements (measurement of deformation of the ballistic material as a result of bullet impact) were made for the first 0-degree shot of each bullet type, which again is consistent with the methods used in the NIJ Standards (-03 and -04 versions). A "V50 ballistic limit" test was conducted on each back armor panel. For the armor models that were originally found compliant with NIJ Standard–0101.04, these V50 values were compared with the baseline V50 obtained during the initial compliance tests. Generally, statistical comparisons of limited V50 are difficult because of the large uncertainties inherent in the ballistic limit test; however, the V50 tests provided further confirmation of a consistent downward shift in ballistic performance for nearly all samples. This "worst-case" testing phase was intended to determine if there was sufficient evidence of performance issues with ZYLON armor taken from the field. The results provided clear evidence of concern with ZYLON-containing body armor although further testing would be needed to confirm the trends observed. Details of the testing and results were reported to the Attorney General. No additional activity is planned under this task.

PHASE II – "LARGE SCALE TESTING"

The scope of the Department of Justice's Body Armor Safety Initiative is much broader than looking at only one model of ZYLON-based armor, and one cannot reliably assume that multiple used vests of the same model will perform similarly because their usage histories and environmental exposures will be different. For this reason, direct application of the NIJ standard for evaluating used armor has always been considered inappropriate. To overcome this limitation, this test program relies on randomly sampling ZYLON-based vests in use around the country and subjecting them to a modified ballistics test protocol that is similar to and consistent with the NIJ test methodology.

The purpose of this broad-based testing phase was to assess the ongoing performance of a broad "cross section" of ZYLON-based body armor in field use. The original plan required the random selection of approximately 500 vests from five different geographic regions of the country, from five different age categories, and from four different manufacturer categories. Because the selection of vests was random, the profile of the sample should look more like a "typical cross section" of what is currently in service. There is no national database relating agencies to specific armor models. The most suitable resource available was the database maintained by the Bureau of Justice Assistance (BJA) to administer the matching funding grants awarded to qualifying agencies under the Bulletproof Vest Partnership (BVP) Grant Act. The limitation of this database is that it includes only those transactions involving agencies that used the matching funds, and not all agencies using ZYLON-containing body armor obtained their body armor with BVP funding. After randomly identifying potential samples in this database, acquiring the field samples involved a concerted effort between NIJ, BJA, NLECTC, and OLES. After establishing broadened policies, the resources of the BVP program were relied upon to obtain body armor in field use and to make arrangements for compensation to participating agencies. In the end, it was possible to obtain only a fraction of the samples originally planned—approximately 75—due to a number of circumstances, but the samples were believed to represent a good cross section of the ZYLON-containing body armor that was still in field service.

Penetration-backface signature ballistics tests were conducted on the test samples using a test protocol similar to that under Phase I, except under Phase II, the armor samples were tested wet. As was the case under Phase I, failure rates obtained from the numerous six-shot armor panel tests were much higher than would have been expected from new armor, thus providing more evidence that the ballistic resistance of most armor models had declined substantially. Specific results were summarized in the Third Status Report to the Attorney General.

Additional V50 ballistic limit tests are planned for the armor models that were originally found compliant with NIJ Standard–0101.04. Armor samples that exhibit large performance shifts will be examined further and compared with those that exhibit little or no significant performance shift. The comparisons will involve applying some of the analytical methods developed under the Applied Research projects to understand if chemical and mechanical changes have occurred to a larger extent in one group.

DELIVERABLES

- Ballistic limit test results on the Phase II armor samples.
- Mechanical and analytical chemical findings on ZYLON extracted from select armor samples.
- Reports that summarize findings.

TESTING OF UPGRADE KITS

One body armor manufacturer offered upgrade kits for use with certain models of body armor. The Body Armor Safety Initiative directed that the performance of these upgrade kits be assessed. Vests that were considered "degraded" were tested with the upgrade kits to determine if the combination of the two consistently prevented bullet penetrations when tested in accordance with the established test protocol. This test effort was completed in early first quarter FY2005, and reported on in a status report to the Attorney General. Briefly, the upgrade kits were found to improve ballistic resistance to some extent, but they did not raise the level of ballistic resistance to the original level intended for each body armor model. No additional activity is planned.

PROJECT: DEVELOPMENT OF METHODOLOGIES FOR SERVICE LIFE PREDICTION AND ACCELERATED TESTING OF SOFT BODY ARMOR

GOALS

To: (1) identify the exposure variables, acting individually or in combination, that initiate performance degradation in soft body armor, (2) identify chemical and physical degradation mechanisms in soft body armor and (3) initiate the development of standardized test protocols for accelerating, predicting, and monitoring the service lives of ballistic fibers and body armor.

Over the last couple of years, research focused on the identification of chemical indicators of PBO fiber tensile strength loss; systematic characterization of PBO fibers; procurement of needed equipment; and development of an experimental design for additional proposed research. Materials analyzed included yarns extracted from: 1) the back panel of the Forest Hills vest that failed in-service, 2) new vests, and 3) virgin spool yarn. In addition to identifying chemical and physical differences between the specimens, this work helped determine which analytical techniques were the most sensitive in detecting chemical changes that reflect subsequent losses in mechanical strength. In particular, Fourier transform infrared (FTIR) spectroscopy was particularly useful in elucidating chemical changes that occurred in the fibers. Evidence of benzamide breakdown, a product of benzoxazole ring-opening, was detected via detailed analysis of the FTIR spectra.

Beginning in 2004 and continuing into 2005, research focused on temperature and moisture aging of PBO ballistic panels in a humidity chamber. Fibers were extracted from the panels at biweekly intervals and tested in tensile mode and analyzed by FTIR. Over the course of the 25 week study, tensile strengths of the extracted yarns decreased ~ 30 % relative to the unaged material, and evidence of significant benzoxazole ring breakage was detected by the FTIR analysis.

A question that arose at the completion of this study was whether residual moisture in the fibers was sufficient to initiate degradation even if the fibers were shielded from external moisture. To help answer this question, a study was conducted in which PBO fibers were hermetically sealed in an inert argon environment in glass tubes and then subjected to the same temperatures as the PBO panels in the previous study. Tensile strengths of the glass-enclosed fibers decreased only a few percent relative to the unaged material.

The remainder of 2005 was focused on the combined effects of temperature, humidity and ultraviolet (UV) exposure on PBO yarns properties. Virgin yarn was placed in specially-designed specimen holders and subjected to a short-term high intensity UV-visible radiation on NIST's Simulated Photodegradation by High Energy Radiant Exposure (SPHERE) system, which is an integrating sphere-based weathering device. Severe degradation (> 50 % decrease) of yarn tensile strength was observed. Preliminary chemical analysis results indicate similar changes in chemistry as observed with the moisture-conditioned specimens; more detailed testing and analyses are in progress.

Customer Needs

Identification and understanding of the phenomena responsible for the loss of mechanical strength in PBO and other ballistic fibers will lead to improvements in the selection of durable and reliable fiers used in body armor. The development of a scientifically-based protocol for screening, testing, and comparing the long-term performance of new and existing fibers for use in ballistic applications will have long term benefts in identifying fibers having improved long-term ballistic performance.

Recent failures of body armor manufactured from PBO fibers have underscored the need to study the service life of these ballistic fibers under a variety of environmental and operating conditions. Manufacturer-supplied data, as well as tests conducted by other commercial research laboratories and governmental labs, have indicated that PBO fiber (which is relatively new in the ballistic armor arena) undergoes degradation in tensile strength following exposure to temperature, moisture and light. Degradation on this level has not yet been observed with more established materials such as Kevlar or Spectra fiber. An extensive and ongoing review of the scientific literature has revealed that neither systematically controlled experiments involving relevant environmental factors, nor detailed chemical analysis of the mechanisms and kinetics of fiber degradation, have yet been carried out. The proposed research will address these issues.

Technical Strategy

Development of scientifically-based accelerated aging and life monitoring protocols for ballistic materials is of vital importance to the body armor industry. Before such development can be undertaken, it is critical that the following issues are addressed:

- The key functional yarn/fiber properties that affect ballistic performance of body armor must be identified, and relevant performance metrics/indices established.

- Key factors in the service environment must be accurately characterized, so that the appropriate test conditions, $e.g.$, temperature, moisture (vapor and condensed), stress amplitude, number of cycles, etc., can be selected and rationally justified.

- A fundamental understanding of the effects of these key factors on degradation mechanisms and kinetics in ballistic fibers/yarns must be obtained.

- Input from key industry players: A NIST workshop is planned to bring key industry players (fiber manufacturers, weavers, vest manufacturers, law enforcement) and members of the NIJ technical working group on body armor together to discuss technical issues associated with accelerated testing/service life prediction including expected vest service life and warranty periods, expected conditions of use, selection of study materials, among others. It is also expected that the workshop will also provide NIST with pertinent information on fiber, fabric, and body armor manufacturing.

LARGER-SCALE STUDIES ARE PLANNED INVOLVING UV, TEMPERATURE, AND HUMIDITY EXPOSURE OF BALLISTIC MATERIALS, IN WHICH CHEMICAL, PHYSICAL, AND MECHANICAL TESTING WILL BE CARRIED OUT AS A FUNCTION OF EXPOSURE

- Molecular Spectroscopy (infrared, UV-visible, X-ray, NMR, Raman): To assess differences in fiber chemistry, $e.g.$, determine if any hydrolysis has occurred, as well as detect possible degradation products or impurities.

- Atomic Spectroscopy (emission spectrometry, atomic absorption spectroscopy): To identify the presence of trace elements such as phosphorus from residual polyphosphoric acid.

- X-ray Diffraction, Neutron Scattering: To determine if any differences in crystallinity or crystal structure exist between various fiber specimens.

- Moisture Absorption (thermogravimetric analysis, moisture sorption analysis): To measure equilibrium moisture content and to measure kinetics of water absorption as a function of temperature and humidity.

- Water and Organic Solvent Extraction: To identify soluble degradation products, fiber additives or sizings, residual polyphosphoric acid, etc., as analyzed by gas chromatography-mass spectrometry (GC-MS) or infrared spectroscopy.
- Dynamic Mechanical Thermal Analysis: To obtain information on fiber modulus, damping and thermal transitions.
- Tensile Testing: To measure the tensile strength, modulus and elongation of the fibers/yarns.

Ballistic materials that will be tested include single fibers, yarns and woven fabrics. Temperatures and relative humidities that span the range of normal use will be used as factors in the study, as well as more extreme temperatures and relative humidities that may be encountered during storage and immersion. UV-visible spectral intensity and UV-visible spectral distribution are also important environmental factors. Of particular interest is to determine and model the degradation kinetics as a function of these environmental factors acting alone and in combination. Another interest is to identify the wavelengths of light that contribute the most to photodegradation, if it is indeed observed. This study will provide information on the antagonistic relationships that could exist between temperature, humidity, UV as well as other environmental and processing variables that are not known at this time.

The results that are obtained will provide critical data necessary for an understanding of the factors responsible for the degradation of ballistic fibers, and will lead to the development of reliable and effective methods for screening and accelerated durability testing.

DELIVERABLES

- Report on chemical analysis of failed and new vests.
- Research reports.

PROJECT: CORRELATION OF FIBER PROPERTIES TO BALLISTIC RESISTANCE

GOALS

To reduce failures of personal body armor by developing tests and standards of assessment for reliability of the active polymeric materials that comprise them. Utilizing the test methods developed in phase I, the research program will be expanded to evaluate the property/performance relationships of other ballistic fibers, such as Kevlar and M5 and the impact of residual processing aids on long-term durability of ballistic fibers. Through the preparation of model fiber systems, the program will be expanded to quantify the link between molecular structure, ballistic performance, and durability. This endeavor will provide a much-needed database of design parameters to facilitate the development of new and more effective ballistic fibers.

CUSTOMER NEEDS

By developing test methodologies that assist in the certification process of protective equipment, the most important outcome of this research will be to save lives.

TECHNICAL STRATEGY

From Phase I of this research project conducted over the last several years it is now known that chemical activity (hydrolytic and UV exposures) and mechanical folding promotes ballistic fiber degradation. Furthermore, new ballistic technologies suggest that ballistic fiber performance and durability are linked to the molecular structure of the polymer. Outputs from Phase I include: (a) A moderately invasive test for evaluating the in service properties of soft body armor. (b) A new device for mechanically degrading yarns, woven fabric, and sections of ballistic armor, and (c) A new methodology for detecting the presence of residual acid.

In Phase I, an armor ballistic performance parameter called U^*, which scales with the V50 velocity of an armor system, was shown to be related to the physical properties of the ballistic fiber [see following equation]. Utilizing this concept, a test methodology was developed that monitors the in service properties of the ballistic fiber by testing fibers from a single strand of yarn. This method still compromises the integrity of the armor panel covering, but only minimally disturbs the ballistic panel structure. The new test methodology has been termed the modified-single fiber test (m-SFT). A journal publication describing the details, reproducibility, and sensitivity of this procedure to mechanical degradation is being prepared.

$$U^* = \frac{\sigma_{uts}\varepsilon_f}{2\rho}\sqrt{\frac{E}{\rho}}$$

[from P. M. Cunniff and M. A. Auerbach, "23rd Army Science Conference," Assistant Secretary of the Army (Acquisition, Logistics, and Technology), Orlando, FL, (December 2002)]

where

σ_{uts} fiber ultimate axial tensile strength

ε_f fiber ultimate tensile strain

ρ fiber density

E fiber modulus (assumed to be linear elastic)

After determining the reproducibility of the procedure, a detailed investigation was initiated using the m-SFT to quantify the degree of degradation of aged and worn vests relative to un-aged vests. The testing is ongoing since the study involves over 1000 samples.

To address the issue of mechanical durability a single 180-degree fold was made in single fiber PBO specimens and evaluated using the m-SFT. The strain-to-failure and ultimate tensile strength of the fibers (i.e., key parameters that quantify the U* parameter) were degraded by approximately 10 %. A device was then designed and built for the repeated folding of ballistic yarns, woven fabric, and sections of ballistic armor (see photo below). Initial results from a fatigued woven yarn indicate that a 20 % drop in the properties of the PBO ballistic fiber may occur within 7 months of wear. A fatigue test is ongoing to simulate longer wear times. Since this is a new testing methodology, a standard folding protocol must be determined.

To determine and quantify the morphological changes that occur during the mechanical folding of ballistic fibers, a special attachment was purchased for the critical dimension – small angle X-ray scattering (CD-SAXS) instrument. Data on virgin fibers shows that the ordered structure of the ballistic fibers can be observed by this approach. Analysis algorithms are currently being written to illuminate morphological changes that occur in damaged ballistic fibers.

PBO and many ballistic fibers are precipitated from concentrated acid solutions (see figure below). Many attempts have been made to unambiguously detect the presence of residual acid and determine the impact of these acids on the hydrolytic degradation of PBO fibers. Complicating this process in PBO is the presence of phosphorus containing processing aids. A test methodology was devised involving the water extraction of acid species coupled with a methylation procedure to facilitate detection. Interestingly, initial results indicate that the water extraction process removed only 25 % of the phosphorus from the fibers, presumably the phosphorus containing processing aids. The fibers are now being manually damaged to facilitate the ingress of moisture into the fibers during the extraction procedure.

The acid research is part of an overall effort to link the chemical degradation mechanisms to changes in the molecular structure of ballistic fibers. The MALDI (matrix assisted laser desorption ionization) technique is being used to detect and quantify these changes in model PBO compounds since

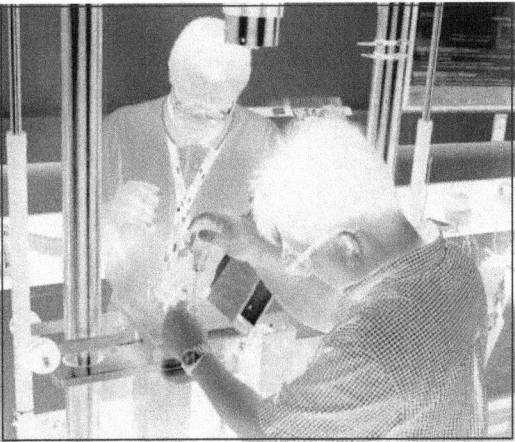

Mechanical Folding Device attached to MTS testing platform being loaded with a piece of woven ballistic fabric.

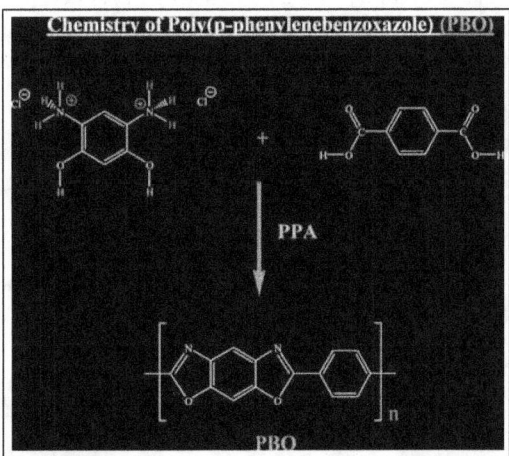

Chemistry of preparation and structure of poly(p-phenylenebenzoxazole) [PBO] fibers. Fibers made from the reaction of 1,3-diamino-4,6-dihydroxybenzene [DADHB] dihydrochloride with terephthalic acid [TA] with poly(phosphoric acid) [PPA] as a catalyst.

ballistic fibers are insoluble in most mediums. In addition, a grinding methodology is being explored to facilitate the detection of insoluble ballistic fibers.

We proposed to complete the degree of aging study currently underway on worn, aged, and un-aged PBO vest and extend the study to include other ballistic fibers. To increase the throughput of this analysis procedure, we will evaluate the feasibly of modifying the Favimat automatic tensile testing device, which is currently being used throughout the fiber industry, to profile the diameter of the tested fiber and measure the fiber displacement.

Utilizing the newly developed mechanical folding device, we propose to standardize on a folding procedure and test all relevant ballistic fibers. The m-SFT will be used to quantify the properties of the tested fibers, since the m-SFT is the best method for quantifying fiber degradation. Therefore, automation of this technique utilizing the Favimat will be critical. The folded fiber region will also be analyzed using the CD-SAXS to quantify morphological changes in the fiber. The mechanical degradation research will be extended to include all ballistic fibers.

In addition to completing the residual acid study, we propose to perform the controlled hydrolytic and UV exposures on PBO model compounds (see figure below for PBO model compounds shown in boxes) and PBO fibers. Initially, MALDI and related preparation procedures will be used to identify and quantify the degradation pathways. The key technical challenge is this research area is the insolubility of the ballistic fiber. As before, this research will be extended to include all relevant ballistic fibers.

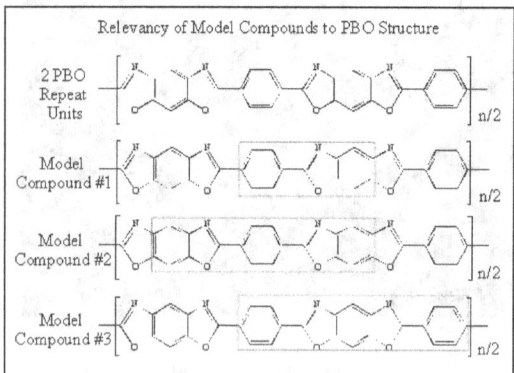

Proposed model compounds (shown in boxes) and their relevancy to the primary structure of PBO fibers.

The continued research into M5, which has been shown to be hydrolytically and UV stable, by Dupont, who also owns Kevlar fibers, and the similarity of the M5 polymer structure to PBO indicates that understanding the impact of molecular structure is the key to developing high performance and environmentally stable ballistic fibers. To predict the performance and durability of these new classes of ballistic fibers, we propose to quantify the impact that molecular modifications have on ballistic fiber performance by having model ballistic fibers prepared that gradually morph the structure of PBO to the environmentally stable M5 polymer. This type of data should facilitate the development of more efficient ballistic fibers while showing the impact of structural modifications on ballistic performance. In addition, understanding the correlation between structure and performance will admit more efficient screening of new fibers targeted for ballistic applications.

DELIVERABLES

- A detailed investigation using the m-SFT of how the physical material properties of worn PBO vests compare with un-aged and laboratory aged vests.

- Initiate and complete similar studies with Kevlar, M5 and other ballistic bers.

- Automate the m-SFT through the use of the ber industry standard Favimat automated testing system. Thereby delivering a protocol that has potential for adoption by industry.

- Assess using PBO ballistic bers the impact of mechanical folding on ballistic performance through the testing of woven fabric, yarns, and/or sections of ballistic material.

- Extend this testing protocol to other ballistic bers.

- Use CD-SAXS to quantify morphological changes in ballistic bers due to mechanical folding.

- Write recommended practice guidelines for the m-SFT testing procedure and the mechanical folding device.

- Determine if phosphoric acid is extractable from PBO bers and quantify its impact on PBO degradation.

- Establish the Hydrolysis and UV-photolysis degradation mechanisms through the use of MALDI, model compounds, chemical modi cation techniques, and relevant analytical techniques.

- Establish a database that quanti es the impact of molecular structural changes on ballistic performance. Morphing the structure of PBO to the M5 ballistic ber will do this.

PROJECT: BALLISTIC LIMIT EVALUATION

GOALS

To improve the implementation of the conventional V50 ballistic limit test so that it can be relied upon as an estimator of armor performance.

CUSTOMER NEEDS

Recent studies of used body armor performance have indicated the need for improved ballistic test methods. Ballistic limit (V50) and penetration-backface signature (P-BFS) testing is currently used to estimate the performance of body armor, but both methods have limitations. P-BFS tests can reliably determine if armor exhibits a certain level of ballistic resistance, but they cannot show if the performance of the body armor has changed, unless the performance has shifted dramatically to unacceptable levels that produce penetrations. V50 ballistic limit tests are more likely to identify modest shifts in performance; however, as the tests are currently performed they can only provide a rough estimate of the ballistic limit and they generally cannot determine how well the armor will perform at the real threat velocities. Furthermore, the uncertainty associated with the estimated V50 value has never been satisfactorily addressed. Improvements in the V50 test and data analysis methods can be incorporated into the NIJ body armor standard and adopted by the armor industry.

TECHNICAL STRATEGY

In 2004 and 2005, research involved analyzing the V50 ballistic limit tests from all NIJ Standard-0101.04 models tested under the NIJ compliance testing program up until that time and fitting the data to a logistic model. The fited data and certain other characteristics of each data series (experimentally determined V50, low complete velocity, zone of mixed results, NIJ reference velocity, etc.) were examined to identify weaknesses and inconsistencies in the current methods. Follow-on studies involved the development of computer simulations to mirror the test protocols employed by test laboratories when they conduct V50 tests. Decision making is guided by the prior ballistic test results, and the armor performance (penetration probability vs. velocity) was modeled as an idealized logistic function. Comparisons were made between the V50 values determined via simulation and the known V50 values used to define the idealized armor performance function.

In 2006, the approach was extended and Monte Carlo methods were used to explore a wide range of armor performance functions and variations in V50 test methods, and improved data analysis methods were implemented. A spreadsheet tool that employs the data analysis methods was also developed for ease of use. The Monte Carlo methods are important because they provide insight that cannot be determined experimentally because other factors interfere with isolating effects of certain key variables. Generally it is recognized that more ballistic testing can lead to a better characterization of the armor, but in the case of V50 testing, understanding how much testing is necessary to achieve reasonable levels of confidence in the results is critical. These simulations have produced estimates of bias and uncertainty associated with the V50 test method, and have proven invaluable in terms of providing evidence to support recommended changes in the amount of testing, in how the data are analyzed, and in how the tests should be performed.

Further studies are planned to determine if the "lower tail" of the armor performance curve can be estimated better using various test strategies. The more favorable strategies will be experimentally demonstrated by testing armor panels or shoot packs.

DELIVERABLES

- Test methodology recommendations.
- Report summarizing research.
- Report of ballistic limit tests demonstrating preferred methods.

PROJECT: CONFORMITY ASSESSMENT PROGRAM DEVELOPMENT

GOALS

To improve the program whereby body armor is tested and certified as "compliant" to the NIJ standard. This effort provides technical support to develop a lab accreditation guide, involvement from the National Voluntary Laboratory Accreditation Program (NVLAP), and expertise from NIST's Technology Services group specializing in Conformity Assessment.

CUSTOMER NEEDS

The ballistic resistance issue that was discovered with used ZYLON-containing body armor has highlighted the importance in improving the process whereby body armor is certified. With the envisioned improvements, there would be greater confidence that future production lots of body armor also complied with the requirements of the standard and that used body armor was still performing as intended.

Technical Strategy

The performance of body armor is presently assessed against the applicable requirements of either:

- Ballistic Resistance of Personal Body Armor (NIJ Standard–0101.04)

- Stab Resistance of Personal Body Armor (NIJ Standard–0115.00)

A key gap inherent in the standards exists because armor is "certified" based on a test of manufacturer-provided samples that are intended to represent production units without any surveillance to provide confidence that production units meet the same minimum performance requirements as the tested samples. Ensuring that future production units comply with these requirements is not addressed by the standard; instead it is the responsibility of the body armor manufacturer to prove, and the purchasing authority to require, that new production units of body armor comply with certain performance requirements. There is much confusion about these issues among vest users and procurement officials.

An initial assessment of the standards and testing program has been made, and an outline for the "Body Armor Certification Program" has been developed. Potential revisions to the current certification program include enhancing the accreditation requirements, audits and assessments of the type-testing laboratories and developing a factory surveillance program to provide confidence that production units continue to meet the performance requirements. The surveillance program will enable the suspension and/or withdrawal of certification of models when continued compliance is in doubt or no longer demonstrated. Audit and assessment of manufacturers' production facilities, quality management system, and inspection of production units are surveillance tools that could be employed in the certification process. NIST intends to work with NIJ to define an improved conformity assessment program and then work with NIJ's certification authority to develop the necessary program documents.

Project: Development and Validation of Short-Term Artificial Aging Protocol for Soft Body Armor

Goals

The project goals are to:

- Use previous research into the chemical and physical degradation of ballistic fibers to develop an interim protocol for artificial aging, suitable for incorporation into the revisions to NIJ Standard–0101.04

- Validate this interim artificial aging protocol by running new ZYLON, Kevlar, and Dyneema vests through it, and then comparing their condition to the condition of used vests.

- Adjust the artificial aging protocol based on the results to allow it to better approximate field aging.

Customer Needs

To comply with the recently modified NIJ requirements for soft body armor (2005 Interim Requirements that became effective September 26, 2005), manufacturers are required to provide evidence that their product(s) will maintain ballistic performance through a declared warranty period. There are significant technical challenges in demonstrating this. As an alternative, the introduction of a consistently applied artificial aging, or "armor pre-conditioning," protocol would provide an objective method for exposing armor to potential damage-causing mechanisms, and successful post-exposure ballistic test results would provide assurance that the armor will maintain acceptable ballistic performance levels under real field conditions. Body armor users and the industry will benefit from this approach because the exposure conditions can be applied consistently and it results in a demonstration that long-term performance requirements are met.

Technical Strategy

In 2003, field failures of body armor manufactured from poly(phenylenebenzobisoxazole) (PBO) fibers brought to national attention the need to study the service life of ballistic fibers under a variety of environmental and operational conditions. The current NIJ standard does not consider environmental factors in vest performance or provide test methods to predict the lifetime of the armor. In order to make an effort to assess the service life of body armor, the first step is to develop a basic artificial aging protocol which will give an approximate idea of body armor performance after exposure to aggressive, but reasonable, use and storage conditions. Then the protocol will be validated by comparison with field return (used) vests.

In early 2006, interactions with industry researchers led to a description of a proposed artificial aging protocol that incorporated elevated temperature, humidity, and mechanical damage as stressing factors. This protocol is based on an engineering assessment of the fundamental conditions influencing armor performance degradation. The protocol continues to be refined and is currently being drafted as a part of the revision to NIJ Standard–0101.04.

Research is planned to perform simple validation tests on the protocol and to allow for adjustments to the test method to better approximate wear in the field. New equipment, including a temperature and humidity chamber and a tumbler, has been set up and the project is awaiting delivery of armor samples. Development of this interim accelerated aging protocol is of vital importance to the body armor industry. The following are crucial components that are being addressed by this research:

- The **effect of tumbling/mechanical damage on vests** will be investigated and guidelines for using tumbling to cause mechanical damage will be developed.

- The **effect of the proposed protocol on new vests** will be established through chemical, physical, and ballistic tests involving vests made from common materials such as Kevlar, ZYLON, and Dyneema. Later, this research will be extended to hybrid armor models.

- **Comparisons must continue to be made between artificially aged vests and used field return vests** to ensure that the damage induced in the artificial aging protocol is reasonable.

- Input from **key industry players**: Collaborations must be established between users, industry, and NIJ/NIST-OLES to acquire materials for these studies.

DELIVERABLES

- Report summarizing the results of validation tests.
- Peer reviewed journal paper on damage effects.
- Final report describing protocol recommended for incorporation into standard.

PROJECT: REVIEW AND UPDATE OF THE BALLISTIC-RESISTANT BODY ARMOR STANDARD

GOALS

To conduct a review of the body armor program and further strengthen the NIJ body armor standard and associated Compliance Testing Program.

CUSTOMER NEEDS

A critical review of the incident in Forest Hills and subsequent discussions with the criminal justice and public safety communities have clearly shown the need for more oversight of ongoing body armor performance and for changes to provide confidence that all body armor produced satisfies certain ballistic performance requirements. To address this, revisions to the ballistic-resistant body armor standard and related compliance testing program are necessary.

TECHNICAL STRATEGY

Consideration was given to input received from public safety agencies, organizations, and associations; manufacturers; and standards and testing organizations. This input coupled with research initiatives underway have led to recommendations to strengthen the ballistic-resistant body armor standard in the following areas: change shot-to-edge distances, revise threat levels, change V50 testing protocols, introduce artificial aging protocols, and test various sizes of body armor. These changes in concert with a more robust conformity assessment program are expected to strengthen the body armor standards and testing program to address the concerns expressed by the criminal justice and public safety communities.

Other efforts planned for the future will investigate additional improvements that could be incorporated into future versions of the standard, such as the development of an improved torso surrogate, introduction of electronic measurements of impact conditions, establishment of requirements of multiple shot resistance, development of contact shot methodologies, and establishment of coverage area requirements.

DELIVERABLES

- Briefings to law enforcement, corrections, public safety, and industry personnel on proposed changes to the NIJ standard and testing program.
- Draft revised body armor standard for comment and review.

PROJECT: BLUNT TRAUMA RESEARCH AND DEVELOPMENT OF AN IMPROVED TEST METHODOLOGY

GOALS

To develop a robust test methodology for evaluating the injury potential from Behind Armor Blunt Trauma (BABT) based on biomechanical studies.

CUSTOMER NEEDS

An area identified in the current NIJ standard requiring further attention is related to test fixturing and the backface deformation performance requirement that is often associated with the threat due to BABT. Deformation of body armor during the ballistic impact event may lead to injuries behind the armor. Though the NIJ standard has been successful in defining a test methodology and performance requirements that led to effective body armor systems, the biomechanical basis for using clay deformation to characterize BABT is uncertain. Unlike the clay, the human thorax is generally viscoelastic, so it is unlikely the response of clay is appropriate for widely varying rates or ranges of deformation. The current test methodology was validated using goat experiments performed over 30 years ago. In addition, the standard does not account for the "penciling effect." This impact does not penetrate the skin, but results in deep deformation over a small area.

Optimization of soft body armor systems requires a more biofidelic coupling of the body armor and the fixture on which it is mounted for testing. Thoracic deformations having the same deformation depths, but different cavity volumes may have significantly different risks of serious injury, and the standard does not address this possibility. In addition, deficiencies identified with the clay system argue for the development of a robust technique for BABT injury assessment. Beyond the existing NIJ standard, there exists no generally accepted injury criterion for thoracic BABT.

TECHNICAL STRATEGY

Two separate efforts have been initiated to address the needs identified. Biokinetics and Associates Ltd. was awarded a contract to develop a torso impact membrane that reproduces the human response for BABT assessment. Development of the enhanced technique for evaluating body armor will involve:

- Engineering of the membrane structure to produce a robust and repeatable physical response that responds in a human-like manner.

- Identification of a relevant engineering measurement, such as force, acceleration, etc. that may be used to quantify the physical response of the torso. The instrumentation is intended to indicate the severity of the ballistic impact.

- Establishment of an injury risk evaluation, which is accomplished by correlating the engineering measurement and an injury model. The injury risk evaluation is expected to be based on mid-thoracic injury tolerance levels. In the NIJ standard, the injury risk evaluation is based on a maximum clay deformation of 44 mm. Under this program, the injury risk evaluation will be based on other quantities obtained from biomechanics research.

- Validation of the injury model, which is accomplished by correlating the injury risk evaluation to a physical model of injury. A meaningful injury risk model must be validated using: 1) epidemiology or physical reconstruction of actual injury events, 2) an animal injury model, or 3) a cadaveric human injury model. Development of a relationship between a robust torso surrogate and a validated injury model is crucial to the success of this approach. The injury model for the NIJ standard includes animal tests that were scaled to human values. Under this program, the injury model will be based on epidemiology and existing injury models established by other biomechanics research programs.

With the development of an instrumented torso surrogate, a two-step process for evaluating body armor will be considered. The potential for bullet penetration would be assessed first on a surrogate with minimal cost risk (*i.e.*, should a penetration occur, valuable instrumentation would not be lost). Following the penetration assessment, further tests on an instrumented surrogate would assess the potential for BABT impact injuries for those body armor systems that pass the penetration tests.

The second research effort supporting this project will provide epidemiological data. This research is being conducted by Wayne State University, which was awarded a contract to study the types of injuries sustained by officers wearing body armor. Study candidates will be identified from the IACP/DuPont Survivors' Club database, and after obtaining approvals, the medical details will be assessed by subject matter experts.

DELIVERABLES

- Torso impact membrane design and test methodology recommendations.
- Report describing epidemiological findings.

Project: Bullet Deformation Behavior

Goals

To provide quantitative measurements of the deformation behavior of commercial bullets that threaten wearers of body armor to improve the ballistic threat assessments used in the NIJ Ballistic-Resistant Body Armor standard.

Customer Needs

An effective body armor standard depends on the ability to accurately characterize the ballistic threats facing officers. The NIJ standard currently specifies bullet velocity, mass, and basic construction (collectively constituting a "threat level"), but it does not address how the material properties of the various bullets, such as strength, ductility and strain rate sensitivity affect their ability to penetrate body armor. These properties can vary among bullets classified in a single threat level category due to different fabrication methods or different alloy compositions used by the various bullet manufacturers. Currently there is no test or means to evaluate the effect of these variations in bullet properties on the performance of body armor.

The customers of this project are those developing and using the NIJ ballistic-resistant body armor standard. This includes modelers who use constitutive models for bullet materials to simulate ballistic impacts on body armor, and government and industry researchers evaluating new threats. Ultimately, the beneficiaries of this work include all who employ body armor for personal protection in the line of duty.

Technical Strategy

Originally this effort began because of concerns over the threat posed by some types of frangible ammunition to soft body armor. "Frangible ammunition" is ammunition loaded with a bullet that is designed to shatter into small pieces upon impact with hard surfaces. Generally this type of ammunition is free of lead, and because of its tendency to shatter upon impact, thereby minimizing the potential for ricochets and collateral damage, it has gained widespread acceptance for use on shooting ranges, training exercises, and in some cases, certain tactical situations. Frangible ammunition is currently used by several government agencies, state and local law enforcement agencies, and other public safety agencies.

Work from various agencies and other groups was reviewed and construction details were researched to better understand differences between various types of frangible bullets. Ballistic tests using different types of frangible ammunition were also conducted against conventional soft body armor. Results suggested that some types of ammunition posed potentially serious problems that were not reflected in the NIJ ballistic-resistant body armor standard. To study this further, efforts were initiated to evaluate the influence of bullet material properties and construction on the penetration ability of the bullet against soft body armor using finite element modeling. However, the high-strain rate mechanical properties necessary for modeling are generally not available. To address this, we began development of a dynamic material properties database for bullet and armor materials, including high rate and heating effects.

Simply measuring the complete set of attributes for every material used in commercially available bullets is prohibitively time consuming and costly. Instead, a simple mechanical test was proposed to quickly evaluate and compare the overall deformation behavior of all commercially-available bullets. This technique was demonstrated on high strain rate mechanical testing of frangible bullets using the NIST Kolsky Bar. A similar approach has been taken to study high-strain rate mechanical properties of individual polymer fibers used in ballistics applications at Purdue University. Results from those mechanical properties tests have supported modeling work on frangible bullet deformation and fracture behavior.

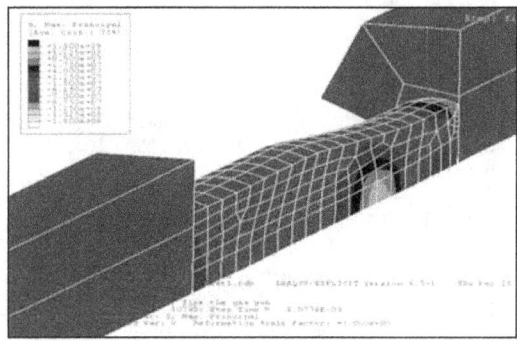

Finite element analysis of a bullet deforming in a Kolsky Bar test. One quarter of the bullet is modeled.

The bullet characterization test subjects bullets to a precise impact load in the NIST Kolsky Bar facility. High speed video cameras capture the deformation of the bullet, and strain gage measurements record the applied force during deformation. The results can then be used to assess whether bullets of a given threat category produced by different manufacturers deform similarly or not. Then detailed metallurgical analyses will be performed on bullets that exhibit unusual deformations, including microstructure, yield stress and strain rate sensitivity measurements. The property data will then be used to predict the deformation observed in the Kolsky Bar tests using finite element analysis. The predictions will reveal the underlying causes of the varied deformation, whether they are due to geometry effects or property differences. The results of this work will enable an improved assessment of the current ballistic threat classification used in the body armor standard and, if necessary, to serve as a basis for developing a new, more useful classification system that would provide a better threat assessment for the next body armor standard.

The Technical Support Working Group is also sponsoring a related effort to examine the ballistic penetration performance of a wide variety of ammunition of interest to law enforcement. That information will become part of a projectile database, and when coupled with constitutive data from this project, will support advanced model development efforts.

DELIVERABLES

Year 1:

- A data set of whole-bullet Kolsky Bar tests, including load vs. time during bullet deformation and video record of bullet deformation for at least 40 bullets from various threat categories and manufacturers.

- Evaluation of data set for consistency of deformation behavior within the existing categories identified in NIJ Standard 0101.04 and identification of possible outliers.

Years 2 and 3:

- Forensic metallurgical analysis of outlier and representative bullets from the same NIJ 0101.04 category.

- Finite element model of deformation of outlier and representative bullet using existing constitutive models of bullet materials as needed to identify possible structural influences on deformation behavior.

- Improved constitutive models for bullet materials based on in-house test data, as needed.

- Final analysis of the deformation behavior of outlier and normal bullets and conclusions as to the primary structural or material behaviors leading to unusual deformation behavior.

- Suggestions for revised categories of ballistic threats and recommended test methods/ characteristic data needed to classify bullets into these new categories for next generation Body Armor Standards.

PROTECTIVE EQUIPMENT PROGRAM

A number of projects are underway to revise other protective equipment performance standards. Similar to the body armor program, the public safety community depends on these standards to assist them in making informed purchasing decisions about important life safety equipment.

PROJECT: NIJ STANDARD–0106.01, "BALLISTIC HELMETS"

GOALS

The objective of this project is to revise the NIJ "Ballistic Helmets" standard and establish new performance levels and test methods based on ballistic impact biomechanics research.

CUSTOMER NEEDS

The new standard will lead to improved helmet designs that will increase the probability of user survivability. It will also provide a standard in which the user community has confidence. Customers will also find that more test laboratories will be able to perform this testing because of changes to the equipment required for testing.

The current NIJ helmet standard is more than twenty years old, was not regularly updated, and was not based on ballistic impact biomechanical principles. Research conducted in the "Study of Head Injuries During Ballistic Loading of Helmets" by the University of Virginia Impact Biomechanics Center (under contract to the U.S. Army Soldier and Biological Chemical Command's Natick Soldier Center (NSC)) indicated that requirements in the existing standard may not ensure adequate protection for individuals wearing ballistic protective helmets meeting the standard. Additionally, relatively few helmets are certified to the existing standard due to a number of reasons: NIJ does not administer a formal Compliance Testing Program for ballistic helmets; the test equipment is difficult to obtain; and the performance levels are outdated and have not kept pace with those defined in the ballistic-resistant body armor standard. The new standard will reduce the risk of serious injury due to ballistic impacts, as well as standardize testing and performance requirements based on modern ballistic impact biomechanical principles.

TECHNICAL STRATEGY

Work will continue under a contract to Biokinetics and Associates Ltd. Numerous issues will be addressed: 1) the current revision only addresses threats up to level II, while existing helmet technologies can readily provide higher levels of protection; 2) the threat definitions in the current revision are different from those in the recently updated ballistic-resistant body armor standard; 3) instrumentation for assessing helmet performance has improved dramatically; and 4) head trauma research has led to a better understanding of injury mechanisms and injury risk criteria. A recently developed ballistic helmet test rig with a load cell module to measure impact loadings will be used to validate the improved test method against a number of commercial and experimental helmet designs. A draft revised standard will be written and sent out for comment and review.

DELIVERABLES

- Report describing validation tests conducted under contract.
- Test equipment and instrumentation.
- Draft revised standard.

PROJECT: NIJ STANDARD–0108.01, "BALLISTIC RESISTANCE OF PROTECTIVE MATERIALS"

GOALS

The objective of this project is to revise the NIJ standard that establishes minimum performance requirements and methods of test for ballistic resistant protective materials.

CUSTOMER NEEDS

Law enforcement agencies rely on the NIJ Standard–0108.01 to ensure the quality and reliability of ballistic resistant materials used for personal protection purposes. These materials are of many types, and can be found in shields, ballistic resistant plates, and vehicle armor.

The current revision of the standard, NIJ Standard–0108.01 was released in September 1985. It added ballistic threat level IIIA and established threat level classifications that were consistent with other NIJ standards for ballistic protection. Since that time, an extensive amount of work was done that led to the NIJ ballistic-resistant body armor standard (NIJ Standard–0101.04), and more recently, the next version of the standard, which is still in draft form. The current NIJ Standard–0108.01 does not reflect any of the improvements that have been introduced into the ballistic resistant body armor standard, and harmonizing the test methods and threat levels of the two ballistic standards is important.

TECHNICAL STRATEGY

Several improvements that have been recommended for the NIJ ballistic-resistant body armor standard will be incorporated into the draft revision of the Ballistic Resistant Materials standard. Improvements include introduction of a V50 ballistic limit test methodology and updating of the ballistic threats. Further clarifications of the scope of the standard are also necessary, and a determination will be made whether to include testing of transparent materials in the revised standard or to develop a separate performance standard for those materials. Additional work is planned to evaluate alternative sample mounting methods, and experimental validation tests of the recommended methods will be conducted.

DELIVERABLES

- Revised draft standard.
- Summary report of validation tests.

PROJECT: NIJ STANDARD–0104.02, "RIOT HELMETS AND FACE SHIELDS"

GOALS

The objective of this project is to revise NIJ Standard–0104.02.

CUSTOMER NEEDS

NIJ Standard–0104.02, "Riot Helmets and Face Shields," was last reviewed in October 1984. Since that time, technological improvements incorporated into helmets and face shields offer better protection, and research has led to a better understanding of head and neck injuries. An improved performance standard that incorporates these considerations into it will allow law enforcement and corrections personnel to specify and procure improved equipment that offers higher levels of protection.

TECHNICAL STRATEGY

Other national standards dealing with helmets were reviewed and comments from practitioners were considered to develop a solicitation seeking a technical contractor to conduct further research leading to a revised draft of the standard. In 2006 a contract was awarded to Biokinetics and Associates Ltd. to conduct research leading to the establishment of a draft standard. Improvements envisioned include revising the threat levels to be consistent with current injury threshold research, requiring the use of ISO headforms, adopting flammability resistance test methods, and giving consideration to the performance of the "tails" protecting the nape. Validation tests are also anticipated to confirm that the test methods can be applied to a fair selection of commercially available riot helmets on the market. The contract duration is 18 months. After delivery of the draft standard, it will be circulated for review and comment by interested parties and then submitted to NIJ for final review and publication.

DELIVERABLES

- Revised draft standard for comment and review.
- Validation test report.
- Finalized revised standard.

ACCOMPLISHMENTS

- Provided technical leadership for the Attorney General's Body Armor Safety Initiative.

- Determined degradation mechanisms responsible for diminished ballistic performance of PBO-containing body armor in field service.

- Drafted a series of reports for the National Institute of Justice that described findings related to the PBO-containing body armor performance assessment.

- Hosted a Body Armor Workshop to inform practitioners and the body armor industry about activities being conducted under the Body Armor Safety Initiative, to discuss ideas under consideration for the next version of the body armor standard, and to solicit feedback from the participants.

- Developed test and measurement methods for assessing changes in PBO and other ballistic materials. Methods are based on assessing certain chemical and mechanical properties.

- Developed specific recommendations for improving the NIJ body armor standard.

- Developed an engineering solution to establish an artificial aging protocol for soft body armor that will be used to pre-condition body armor before ballistic certification testing, thus providing increased confidence that the body armor will maintain intended ballistic performance levels after it is pressed into field service.

- Initiated the establishment of a robust conformity assessment program for body armor, but which could also be applied to other equipment certification programs.

- Developed improved test methodologies for assessing ballistic helmets.

PUBLICATIONS

Forster, A. L., Chin, J. W., Gundlach, M., "Effect of Bending and Mechanical Damage on the Physical Properties of Polybenzobisoxazole (PBO) Fiber." Polymer Preprints (in press).

Chin, J. W., Forster, A. L., Rice, K. "Temperature and Moisture Aging of Polybenzobisoxazole Fibers." Polymer Preprints (in press).

G. A. Holmes, K. Rice, and C. R. Snyder. "Ballistic Fibers: A Review of the Thermal, Ultraviolet and Hydrolytic Stability of the Benzoxazole Ring Structure."*Journal of Materials Science* **41**(13), 4105-4116 (2006).

U.S. Department of Justice report, "Third Status Report to the Attorney General on Body Armor Safety Initiative Testing and Activities." *NCJ 210418*, (August 24, 2005).

J. Chin, E. Byrd, A. Forster, X. Gu, T. Nguyen, W. Rossiter, S. Scierka, L. Sung, P. Stutzman, J. Sieber, and K. Rice. "Chemical and Physical Characterization of Poly(p-phenylene benzobisoxazole) Fibers Used in Body Armor." *NISTIR 7237*, (March 2005).

U.S. Department of Justice report, "Status Report to the Attorney General on Body Armor Safety Initiative Testing and Activities." *NCJ 204534*, (March 11, 2004).

U.S. Department of Justice report, "Supplement I: Status Report to the Attorney General on Body Armor Safety Initiative Testing and Activities." *NCJ 207605*, (December 27, 2004).

S. P. Mates, R. Rhorer, S. W. Banovic, E. Whitenton, and R. J. Fields. "High Rate Tensile Strength Measurements of Frangible Bullets using a Kolsky Bar." in Proceedings of the 2006 SEM Annual Conference and Exposition on Experimental and Applied Mechanics, June 4-7 2006, St. Louis, MO, USA.

S. W. Banovic. "Microstructural Characterization and Mechanical Behavior of Cu-Sn Frangible Bullets." Submitted to Material Science and Engineering A.

PRESENTATIONS AND POSTERS

NIJ JUICE Session July 2006, Washington, DC "Artificial Aging Protocols" (Presentation).

NIJ Body Armor Technical Working Group Meeting, Washington DC, April 2006 "Short Term Artificial Aging Protocols for Incorporation into the Revised NIJ 0101.04 Body Armor Standard" (Presentation).

American Chemical Society, Atlanta GA, March 2006 "Effect of Bending and Mechanical Damage on the Physical Properties of Polybenzobisoxazole (PBO) Fiber" (Presentation).

DETECTION, INSPECTION, AND ENFORCEMENT TECHNOLOGIES

As America's homeland security efforts to detect, locate, and interdict threats intensify, the work of OLES' Detection, Inspection and Enforcement Technologies program becomes increasingly important.

This program has been continually improving the NIJ standards for walk-through and hand-held metal detectors. Two continuing projects focus on testing and improving the capabilities of current walk-through metal detectors (WTMDs) and hand-held metal detectors (HHMDs). The latest revision of HHMD standard, NIJ Std-0602.03, was recently completed. This revision updated the requirements and improved one of the test methods. The next step is to establish an NIJ test and evaluation program for this standard. The WTMD standard is also being revised. The changes will include updating the requirements, as was done with the HHMD standard, and revising several test procedures bearing in mind the cost of test cannot be prohibitively expensive. One issue, common to both HHMD and WTMD testing, is the materials used to fabricate the test objects. Although the geometry and material specifications are accurately defined, this does not guarantee the electromagnetic properties of the test objects are reproducible, which is important for device assessment. Consequently, we are testing a sample of metals to get mean values and lot-to-lot and between-manufacturer variations for the appropriate electromagnetic properties. In addition, human phantoms will be developed to emulate the electromagnetic properties of humans, thereby removing the last nonquantitative test from the standards.

A draft of the NIJ standard for the portable X-ray systems used by bomb technicians to identify improvised explosive devices and subsequently plan strategies for their interdiction has been recently completed. This revision introduces mechanical tolerance, electromagnetic immunity, and environmental tolerance requirements. Another revision has been started to address imaging quality requirements. Presently, the image quality requirement is not rigorous nor does it lend itself to objective evaluation. We plan on separating this requirement into several metrics that can be objectively evaluated. We are also examining the possibility of establishing protocols for including the effects of human perception in these requirements.

This year, the Detection, Inspection and Enforcement Technologies program started a new and broad program in imaging quality as applied to systems and devices used by emergency responder, law enforcement, criminal justice, and security providing agencies. Thus far, this program includes developing minimum performance requirements for the X-ray backscatter systems used for personnel screening, the portable X-ray systems as mentioned above, the infrared cameras used by firefighters, visible-light digital video cameras used by police and other agencies performing surveillance, and radio-frequency through-wall surveillance and imaging systems. Each of these activities has unique requirements for evaluating the performance of the imager, including for example, unique test objects and test scenarios. This will be discussed in detail below.

Three activities are presently being supported for detection of concealed objects. This includes two passive imaging systems, one directed to short stand-off (1 m to 5 m) imaging in both indoor and outdoor environments and with sufficient thermal resolution to allow rapid acquisition rates (> 20 fps), and the other dedicated to long stand-off (to 100 m) for suicide bomber detection. Both

Technical Contacts:
Nicholas Paulter
Donald Larson

Staff-Years:
7

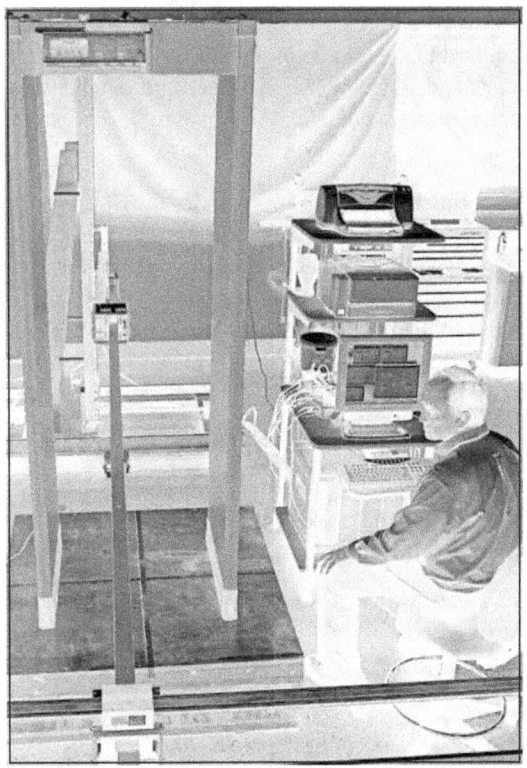

systems use cyro-cooled detector technology, which has become a commercially-viable solution in the last few years because of the development of related medical imaging technology. The short stand-off system uses standard silicon technology thereby significantly reducing the cost of the arrays relative to presently-available indium-phosphide-based detectors and associated low-noise amplifiers. The long stand-off system will leverage the now-mature and reliable technology developed by NIST for astronomical research. The third activity is the development of a pulsed terahertz system based on optical pulse generation and sampling techniques.

The Detection, Inspection, and Enforcement Technologies program is also developing evaluation standards for advanced human recognition systems that will allow qualitative performance testing of recognition products over a wide range of watch-list and access-control applications.

In the enforcement arena, standards for traffic speed measuring devices are constantly being updated to keep pace with the enhancements manufacturers introduce into their products to improve the ability of law enforcement officers to catch speed offenders on our nation's highways and roads. In addition, a new standard is being prepared for detection systems that capture information of light violations at traffic-light controlled intersections.

Project: NIJ Standard–0601.02, "Walk-Through Metal Detectors for Use in Concealed Weapon and Contraband Detection"

Goals

To continue improving the latest revision of the Walk-Through Metal Detector (WTMD) performance standard, design and implement improvements to the robot used for WTMD performance tests, and provide technical assistance in the establishment of the NIJ Compliance Testing Program.

Customer Needs

Increasing attention is being given to checkpoint security, and great confidence is placed in walk-through metal detectors to detect items that might pose a threat to public safety. Routinely, one can find WTMDs being used to screen correctional facility populations and their visitors, as well as to screen people for admission to airport terminals, courthouses, schools, sports stadiums, amusement parks, and political events, and this is only a partial list. It is essential for the WTMD to be adjusted properly to sense the types of threat objects of interest, and that it performs this detection function accurately and reliably. The WTMD performance standard fills an important void in that it is the only reference developed specifically for these products that ties together many important performance requirements (electrical safety and vulnerability, electromagnetic compatibility, detection performance, and environmental resistance).

Historically, WTMD manufacturers were not compelled to design their products to meet a broad array of performance requirements, but rather only a subset of requirements to meet basic electrical safety and perhaps electromagnetic emissions requirements. In consultation with a group of industry, users, and government representatives, OLES developed what has now become the current version of the NIJ "Walk-Through Metal Detector" performance standard, NIJ Standard–0601.02. A formal WTMD Compliance Testing Program based on this standard was initiated in mid-FY2002 and completed in FY2003. NIST worked closely with the National Law Enforcement and Corrections Technology Center (NLECTC) and a commercial test laboratory to implement the WTMD Compliance Testing Program, through which several models of commercially available WTMDs were tested. This test program has proven very valuable, both in terms of generating data on products of interest and in terms of pinpointing areas in the standard that could be improved further. Comments and suggestions for further improvements to the standard were, and continue to be, collected from industry.

Since the first series of tests under the Compliance Testing Program, numerous requests have been made by manufacturers and procurement authorities to have units tested against the standard. Presently there are no commercial laboratories recognized by NIJ to do this. This project will start on the next revision of the standard and provide the technical support needed to implement an ongoing Compliance Testing Program.

Technical Strategy

■ Provide technical support to NIJ and the NLECTC, which will administer the Compliance Testing Program, for re-establishing the testing program.

■ Revise standard, including the following: 1) revise test procedures; 2) update references to other standards; and 3) revise performance requirements.

- Publish the new test objects document that includes fabrication details for the test object, materials of construction, and required test orientations.

- Modify the OLES robot. Of special interest is the addition of hardware to minimize test object bounce and to improve positional accuracy. Software modifications are also planned to improve the measurement process.

DELIVERABLES

- Revised standard.
- Separate test objects document.
- Administrative manual for test program.
- Compliance test report form.

PROJECT: NIJ STANDARD–0602.02, "HANDHELD METAL DETECTORS FOR USE IN CONCEALED WEAPON AND CONTRABAND DETECTION"

GOALS

To implement the latest revision of the Hand-Held Metal Detector (HHMD) performance standard, and provide technical assistance to the NIJ's Compliance Testing Program.

CUSTOMER NEEDS

Hand-held metal detectors are often used to supplement the interrogation provided by walk-through metal detectors (WTMDs), especially if the WTMD gives a positive alarm. The HHMD allows the security screener to pinpoint areas of primary concern and to inspect them more closely to detect items that might pose a threat to public safety. These devices are found nearly everywhere that WTMDs are found, and they are often the last inspection devices used to screen someone; therefore, it is critical that they perform their intended function accurately and reliably. As is the case with WTMDs, manufacturers of HHMDs were not compelled to design their products to meet a broad array of performance requirements, but this standard and a coordinated Compliance Testing Program will fill that void.

In consultation with a group of industry, users, and government representatives, OLES has developed a draft revision of the NIJ "Hand-Held Metal Detector" performance standard, which will be NIJ Standard–0602.03. Both manufacturers and users have requested establishment of a sustainable test program through which HHMD performance can be certified. A formal Compliance Testing Program based on this standard has not been initiated.

With the new revision of the standard and the establishment of a Compliance Testing Program, manufacturers will be able to assess their designs against the full array of performance requirements, make adjustments to improve their designs to address vulnerabilities that might be exposed during testing, and allow users of HHMDs to purchase compliant products with confidence. The standard has been used by quality manufacturers as a developmental aid to achieve improved HHMD performance.

The current activities of this project are to publish the draft revision of the NIJ standard and to provide the technical support required to implement an ongoing Compliance Testing Program.

TECHNICAL STRATEGY

- Provide technical support to NIJ and NLECTC, which will administer the Compliance Testing Program. Assist in identification of laboratories that can conduct the tests in the standard and work closely with NLECTC to implement the HHMD Compliance Testing Program.

- Publish the new test objects document that includes fabrication details for the test object, materials of construction, and required test orientations.

DELIVERABLES

- Revised standard.
- Identification of laboratories.
- Test objects document.
- Administrative manual for test program.
- Compliance test report form.

PROJECT: EVALUATION OF BIOMETRIC RECOGNITION SYSTEMS

GOALS

To design methods for the evaluation of systems and technologies that identify humans in imagery and promote and advance face recognition technology designed to support existing face recognition efforts in the U.S. Government. Questions to be addressed include: has face recognition technology performance improved by an order of magnitude since the last formal independent evaluation; how well does it perform based on different image/video quality levels? Is there correlation with other biometrics such as iris? This technology will improve public services and benefit law enforcement and homeland security applications.

CUSTOMER NEEDS

In prior fiscal years, NIST has been funded to conduct data gathering efforts, which have resulted in a human identification database. Using the database, NIST has developed the measurement methods for analyzing performance of facial recognition systems. The methods have proven sufficiently generic such that iris recognition systems can be evaluated in much the same manner. Indeed the measurement techniques and performance statistics are applicable to a wide range of biometrics, and non-human recognition tasks.

This effort is funded by the National Institute of Justice. Several image databases have been used for the NIST face tests. First, a NIST-gathered collection of volunteer images constitutes a database of multi-modal, multi-site, and multi-biometric collection. Second, 6.8M operational images from the Department of State give very large-scale performance numbers that are predictive of deployed performance in visa processing applications. Two additional databases collected at other government and academic facilities contain multi-modal images and video streams that can be used to test correlation between various biometric applications.

This effort will lead to increased efficiency and accuracy of verification/identification systems; allow quantitative performance testing of human recognition technology over a wide range of watch-list and access-control applications.

This project represents a continuation of the face and iris recognition evaluation projects that are anticipated to continue for at least another year. Emphasis will be on analyzing current evaluation results, measuring performance on various quality levels, and conducting correlation testing with other biometric modalities. An additional emphasis on performance from high and low quality video is anticipated.

These independent and unbiased technical evaluations are activities to which NIST is uniquely qualified. Related activities at NIST include face recognition technology development, evaluation of iris recognition, and mandated certification of government face recognition systems under the US Patriot Act.

TECHNICAL STRATEGY

NIST will conduct a series of independent, government evaluations on face and iris recognition and analyze the results to measure improved performance accuracy and correlation between biometric modalities.

NIST will administer the Facial Recognition Verification Test (FRVT) 2006 and the Iris Challenge Evaluation (ICE) 2006 independent Government evaluations and write the final report for the Face Recognition Grand Challenge (FRGC).

NIST will administer the FRVT 2006 and the ICE 2006 independent Government evaluations, analyze the results and write the final reports.

DELIVERABLES

- A summary report will be written upon the completion of each biometric evaluation. The nal report on the FRGC is to be completed by the end of the fourth quarter.

PROJECT: FAST CAPTURE EVALUATION

GOALS

To evaluate fast capture devices for collecting rolled-equivalent fingerprints being developed under grants awarded by NIJ. Questions to be addressed include: does the device effectively capture fingerprints; with what speed; at what resolution, with what quality; and are the fingerprints captured compatible with legacy fingerprint systems and repositories? These devices promise an order of magnitude decrease in capture time, making it more efficient to collect rolled fingerprints from subjects. This technology, if proven, will improve public services and benefit law enforcement and homeland security applications.

CUSTOMER NEEDS

Tenprint capture technology today on average requires (under ideal circumstances) around 3 minutes to process a subject. New fast capture technologies promise complete tenprint capture on the order of 10 seconds.

Legacy fingerprints and systems have been designed to process inked fingerprint cards that have been scanned and live scan fingerprint images. To date, hundreds of millions of prints have been collected and enrolled into systems such as the FBI IAFIS and DHS IDENT. The sensor technologies being applied in this fast capture initiative are considerably different. These include contactless sensors and photographic capture of friction skin detail. Tests are required to determine the quality of fingerprint images produced by these new devices and their compatibility with legacy fingerprint systems and repositories.

This project represents a new activity that is anticipated to go on for at least two years. These NIST evaluations are commencing at the end of the first year of NIJ funding to grant awardees, and the evaluations are expected to continue through at least the end of a second year of NIJ funding.

These independent and unbiased technical evaluations are activities to which NIST is uniquely qualified. Related activities at NIST include mandated certification of government fingerprint systems under the US Patriot Act, and mandated testing and certification for PIV, which include the development and standardization of a fingerprint image quality algorithm along with SDK fingerprint matcher tests.

This effort will lead to increased efficiency and accuracy; increased latent search ability improving prosecutions and forensic investigations.

TECHNICAL STRATEGY

NIST will receive prototype devices on loan from NIJ and conduct a series of investigative tests to evaluate the fingerprint images produced by these devices. Factors to be studied include: fingerprint image quality, fingerprint compatibility, capture speed, and device usability. It should be noted that this project will not include any large-scale data collection.

DELIVERABLES

- A summary report will be written and given to NIJ upon the completion of each device evaluation. Quarterly reports and an annual report will be provided

PROJECT: TECHNOLOGIES FOR TRAFFIC ENFORCEMENT

GOALS

To develop and maintain performance specifications that assure the accuracy and reliability of speed-measuring devices and systems used by law enforcement, and to assist the International Association of Chiefs of Police (IACP) with administering an independent testing program from which a products list for each type of speed-measuring device is maintained.

CUSTOMER NEEDS

Police traffic radar devices have been used in this country to detect speeding motorists since the 1940s. Since then, radar devices have evolved from clumsy, stationary models into sophisticated, microprocessor-enhanced units capable of monitoring vehicle speeds in either direction from moving patrol cars, and into automated across-the-road systems that automatically capture images of speed-offending vehicles. The successful application of radar technologies to speed enforcement has spawned interest in the development of laser technologies, such as lidar devices and photolidar systems that photographically document speed violations, as well as an interest in intersection safety systems that record red light violations. Against this bewildering array of technically complex speed-enforcement tools, law enforcement administrators are forced to make difficult procurement decisions.

TECHNICAL STRATEGY

Through the development of minimum performance standards, and testing programs administered by the IACP, baselines are established for acceptable device and system performance. This gives courts and law enforcement officers assurance that those product models, determined by test to comply with the specifications, will provide accurate and defensible information.. To further this program, it is recommended that equipment buyers incorporate these performance specifications into their procurement documents, requiring that units offered for purchase meet or exceed the requirements of the performance specifications. This is intended to encourage manufacturers to produce better devices and systems. Since device features are constantly evolving, the specifications are subjected to continuing review.

DELIVERABLES

- Maintenance of up-to-date minimum performance specifications for traffic speed-measuring devices and systems.
- Development of an intersection safety system standard.
- Assistance to the IACP with administration of its device and system Compliance Testing Program.

PROJECT: IMAGING METROLOGY

This general program is directed to the development of metrology for a broad range of imaging technologies used in security, surveillance, and evidence-gathering applications. Although the imaging systems may use different sensor technologies, such as X-ray, infrared, visible light, and radio frequency sensors, there are many common requirements that can be addressed simultaneously. The common components include, for example, display quality, human-in-the-loop, the effects of algorithmic processes, and dissemination of the measurement capability to qualified testing laboratories.

GOALS

To develop a comprehensive imaging system characterization program that will result in test methods, systems, and metrics to evaluate the performance of each component in an imaging system, including image acquisition device, encryption/decryption and compression/decompression algorithms, recording devices, display devices, and transmit and receive devices as necessary for wireless image transfer; to assess the performance of the entire video system as defined by the user; and to assess the efficacy of automatic recognition software.

CUSTOMER NEEDS

Presently there are no quantifiable and reproducible methods for assessing the imaging performance of imaging systems used by first responder, law enforcement, and criminal justice agencies. Users of this equipment are forced to rely upon manufacturer claims and comparisons. Furthermore, there is no traceable or reference on which to base a technical comparison of imaging technology and/or systems.

TECHNICAL STRATEGY

The list below is in order of increasing wavelength of the electromagnetic energy used by the imaging system.

- X-ray personnel screeners (backscatter and transmission systems). These are the personnel screening systems being considered for deployment at security checkpoints or that have been deployed for evaluation.

    – Work in collaboration with manufacturers, users, and other government agencies to develop minimum requirements for imaging performance, which will become IEEE/ANSI Std. N42.47.

- X-ray portable package imagers (pulsed, cw, and dual energy). These are the portable X-ray imaging devices use by bomb squads to identify bombs in leave-behind packages and to plan appropriate interdiction strategies.

    – Work in collaboration with the International Association of Bomb Technicians and Investigators (IABTI), bomb squads across the nation, and manufacturers to develop the second revision of the National Institute of Justice (NIJ) Standard, 0603.02, which will address imaging performance requirements.

    – Develop appropriate transfer standards.

    – Establish laboratory facility for assessing applicability of imaging requirements and ability of systems to meet these requirements.

    – Develop objective performance metrics that include the effect of human perception on imaging performance.

- Visible, digital video camera. These are the camera systems that will soon be replacing the analog video systems used in a plethora of security, surveillance, and evidentiary applications. The imaging system may include several components that are not part of the camera but are important for the utility of the imaging system for their targeted purposes. Applications of this work includes police in-car video, perimeter/site security, and general surveillance.

    – Develop minimum performance requirements, in collaboration with manufacturers and users.

    – Develop test methods and standards for evaluating requirements.

    – Develop visible-light complex scene projector.

        o White-light source, pixel-level control of light spectrum and intensity

        o Frames rates > 20 fps

    – Develop reference test bed from which to accredit third-party labs.

- Infrared (IR) digital cameras. These are the camera systems that will be replacing and have replaced analog cameras in security, surveillance, and emergency response applications. Applications that will be addressed include the cameras used by firefighters to find downed people inside of collapsing and burning structures and to assess conditions within burning structures. The firefighter cameras have unique requirements relative to conventional IR cameras in that they are exposed to high temperatures, a small temperature differential between target object and background, and the requirement for automatic control of certain functions. The unique requirements will also be addressed.

- Develop minimum performance requirements, in collaboration with manufacturers and users.

- Develop test methods and standards for evaluating requirements.

- Develop IR complex scene projector.

    o Monochromatic source, pixel-level control of light intensity

    o Frames rates > 20 fps

- Develop reference test bed from which to accredit third-party labs.

DELIVERABLES

- Prototype visible-light complex scene projector.
- Prototype IR complex scene projector.
- List of performance metrics for IR imager.
- List of performance metrics for in-car digital video system.
- List of imaging performance metrics for portable X-ray systems.
- List of imaging performance metrics for personnel screener X-ray systems.

Project: Through-Wall Imaging and Surveillance

Imaging and surveillance are two different functions and operations for through-wall systems. Whereas imaging requires information appropriate for recognition of objects, surveillance does not. Surveillance may, for example, be based on motion of objects. More than likely, because of the physical principles involved and size and cost restrictions for a system, imaging will likely be a short-standoff (less than 20 m) operation and surveillance will be a long stand-off (up to 1000 m) operation.

Goals

To develop functionally agile and programmable reference through-wall system on which the performance of commercially-available systems can be assessed and on which to base the development of applicable minimum performance standards and a reference measurement test bed.

Customer Needs

Law enforcement and military have long required the ability to determine the occupancy of structures at a safe distance and to be able to track motion of several occupants simultaneously. Furthermore, once a structure has been identified as necessary to breach or to surveil with greater detail, the law enforcement and military personnel require images of sufficient accuracy to infer the intent or disposition of the occupants.

Several manufacturers have recently made available through-wall systems for imaging and surveillance to meet the above requirements. However, there are no minimum performance standards for these systems and the user, consequently, must rely solely on the manufacturers' claims regarding the performance of these systems. The users need established standards on which to base comparative studies and/or to make an objective performance assessment.

Technical Strategy

■ Establish collaboration with industry to develop a reference through-wall imaging system for short stand-off distances using non-mechanical sub-5-GHz scanning systems.

■ Establish collaboration with the US military and contractors to develop a reference through-wall surveillance system for long stand-off distances using stepped multi-band radar technology.

■ Develop accurate methods for measuring the broadband electromagnetic properties of building materials and then to apply these techniques to assess the electromagnetic properties of prepared building materials. Use the data to create a NIST-traceable measurement database.

■ Design reference test bed, including walls, human phantoms, clutter, and targets for assessing performance of through-wall systems.

■ Initiate development of human phantoms for the 200 MHz to 10 GHz frequency range.

DELIVERABLES

- Electromagnetic property measurements for a wide spectrum of building materials, including concrete and rebar, over a broad range in frequency.
- The fabrication, analysis and experimental testing of a number of accurate, non-destructive RF and microwave measuring systems.
- A database of dielectric materials.
- Publications in the form of NIST Technical Notes and/or articles in professional journals.

Project: Concealed Weapon Detection and Imaging

Goals

To develop imaging systems that can be used to find objects concealed under clothing at distances from 1 m to 100 m.

Customer Needs

Law enforcement and military personnel require the ability to identity suicide bombers at long stand-off distances (to 100 m) and smaller weapons (handguns and knives) at shorter stand-off distances (1 m to 5 m).

Technical Strategy

- Develop a real-time (>20 frames/s) imaging system that can be used to detect large concealed objects for identifying suicide bombers at distances up to 100 m. The imaging will use a staring array developed by NIST for astronomical research over that last couple decades.

- Develop a hyperspectral imaging system using short pulsed lasers and optoelectronic devices to provide images of the contents of optically opaque containers and packages, and to provide spectral identification capability for certain classes of organic materials hidden inside these containers.

Accomplishments

- Two new staff were added: a new program manager and an electronics engineer.

- Established hand-held metal detector and walk-though metal detector test bed.

- Redesigned the metal detector test robot to accommodate heavy test objects, laser positioning of test objects, automatic test object parameter selection, etc.

- Draft document describing metal detector test objects.

- Proposed revision of NIJ hand-held metal detector (HHMD) standard, NIJ Std-0602.03.

- Draft compliance test report form for hand-held metal detectors.

- Draft administrative manual for HHMD test program.

- The HHMD robotic tester was successfully used to test six HHMDs by an inexperienced outside operator with minimal training (less 2 hrs).

- Draft revision of NIJ portable X-ray standard, NIJ Std-0603.01.

- Started development of test bed for evaluation of portable X-ray systems.

- Established an ad hoc group of industry, user, and government representatives to address imaging quality requirements of NIJ's portable X-ray standard.

- Initiated and led review of IACP's sampling process for testing traffic enforcement devices.

- The basic metrology underlying the measurement of materials for security applications and a list of the dielectric parameters of a large number of commonly-used materials was written and published, Technical Note 1536 (150 pages): "Measuring the permittivity and permeability of lossy materials: Solids, liquids, metals, building materials, and negative index materials," Feb. 2005.

- Developed and extended the shielded-open-circuit holder method to use 7 mm diameter coaxial transmission lines, and have investigated the use of 3.5 mm coaxial line, to extend our liquid measurement capability. This work allows us to obtain measurements on many liquids from 1 MHz to 10 GHz. This work is being summarized in a paper that will be submitted to an IEEE journal.

- A generalized polarization model that yields material relaxation times from dielectric measurements was developed from basic statistical mechanics. This model helps describe the unique permittivity signatures of materials in the radio-frequency and microwave bands. This work has been summarized in a publication submitted to Physical Review.

- Determined that making a digital recording of the composite video (CV) output signal of the thermal imagers is not necessarily a good indicator of the performance of the entire imaging system (which includes the electronic visual display of the device). The transfer function between the CV and the image displayed by the video display may not be flat, and varies from imager to imager.

- Fabrication of the antenna-coupled microbolometer (ACMB) arrays for use in the close-proximity CWD imaging system was successfully outsourced to commercial foundry. This is a major step because now the arrays can be fabricated at an implied cost of less $ 15/channel (unpackaged) compared to almost $1000 for the competitive detector technology, indium phosphide detectors and low-noise amplifiers.

- The spectral response of the ACMB detectors was measured to be between 0.1 THz and 1.5 THz.

- ACMB detector performance was verified in a refrigerated (cryogen-free) platform.

- The performance of the ACMB array modules, which are 8-element modules, was verifed. These modules will be assembled to provide the array size and arrangement appropriate for given CWD applications.

- For the long stand-off CWD system using transition-edge sensors (TESs), the optics design was completed and the optical path has been fully simulated.

- The room-temperature electronics for the TES array readout is being fabricated and assembled.

- The Face Recognition Grand Challenge, a technology development project facilitated by NIST.

- Preliminary results show an order of magnitude improvement over FRVT 2002 results.

- Facial Recognition Vendors Test 2000 and 2002, www.frvt.org.

- Supplemental report on FRVT 2002, released January 2004.

- October 2003, New color, high resolution, release of the FERET face database (superseding the greyscale version 500 copies of which were issued between February 2001 and September 2003); http://www.itl.nist.gov/iad/humanid/feret/.

PUBLICATIONS

J. Baker-Jarvis, M. D. Janezic, B. F. Riddle, R. T. Johnk, P. Kabos., C. Holloway, R. G. Geyer, and C. A. Grosvenor, *Measuring the Permittivity and Permeability of Lossy Materials: Solids, Liquids, Metals, Building Materials, and Negative-Index Materials*," NIST Technical Note 1536, February 2005.

J. Baker-Jarvis, B. Riddle, and M. D. Janezic, "Polarization Evolution, Relaxation Times, and the Local Field," submitted for publication, Phys. Rev.

F. Amon, A. Hamins, and J. Rowe, "First responder thermal imaging cameras: establishment of representative performance testing conditions," SPIE Defense and Security Symposium, 17 – 20 April 2006, Orlando, FL, paper 6205-37.

F. Amon, and A. Hamins, "First responder thermal imaging cameras: development of performance metrics and test methods," SPIE Defense and Security Symposium, 17 – 20 April 2006, Orlando, FL, paper 6207-28.

J. B. Dinaburg, F. Amon, A. Hamins, and P. Boynton, "LCD display screen performance testing for handheld thermal imaging cameras," SPIE Defense and Security Symposium, 17 – 20 April 2006, Orlando, FL, paper 6207-29.

F. Amon and N. Bryner, "Advances in thermal imaging technology in the first responder arena," SPIE Defense and Security Symposium, 17 – 20 April 2006, Orlando, FL, paper 6207-32.

S. W. Brown, J. P. Rice, J. D. Jackson1, J. E. Neira, and B.C. Johnson, "Spectrally tunable sources for advanced radiometric applications," submitted to J. Res. Nat'l. Inst. Stands. Technol.

J. P. Rice, S. W. Brown, B. C. Johnson and J. E. Neira, "Hyperspectral image projectors for radiometric applications," Metrologia, Vol. 43, 2006, pp. S61–S65.

J. P. Rice, S. W. Brown, and J. E. Neira, "Development of hyperspectral image projectors," SPIE Optics and Photonics, 14 - 15 August 2006, Sand Diego, CA, paper 6297-01.

S. W. Brown, J. P. Rice, J. E. Neira, R. Bousquet, and B. C. Johnson, "Hyperspectral Image Projector for Advanced Sensor Characterization," SPIE SPIE Optics and Photonics, 14 - 15 August 2006, Sand Diego, CA, paper 6292-02.

A. Luukanen, E. N. Grossman, and A. J. Miller, "A Superconducting bolometer for THz imaging," submitted to IEEE Microwave and Wireless Components Letters.

C. Dietlein, A. Luukanen, Z. Popovic, and E. Grossman, "A W-band Polarization Converter and Isolator," submitted to IEEE Microwave and Wireless Components Letters.

A. Luukanen, E. N. Grossman, A. J. Miller, P. Helistö, J. S. Penttilä, H. Sipola,, H. Seppä, "An Ultra-Low Noise Superconducting Antenna-Coupled Microbolometer with a Room-Temperature Read-Out," IEEE Microwave and Wireless Components Letters, Vol.16, No. 8, August 2006, pp. 464 – 466.

P. Helistö, A. Luukanen, L. Grönberg, J. S. Penttilä1, H. Seppä, H. Sipola1, C. R. Dietlein, and E. N.Grossman, "Antenna-coupled microbolometers for passive THz direct detection imaging arrays," Proceeding of European Microwave Conf. 2006, 10 – 15 Sept. 2006, Manchester, UK.

A. Luukanen, A. J. Miller, and E. N. Grossman, "Passive hyperspectral terahertz imagery for security screening using a cryogenic microbolometer," Proc. SPIE, 17 – 18 Apr. 2006 Bellingham, WA, paper 62120Y.

C. Dietlein, A. Luukanen, F. Meyer, Z. Popovic, and E. Grossman, "Phenomenology of Passive Broadband Terahertz Images," Proceedings of Fourth ESA Workshop on Mmw technology and applications, Noordwijk, NL, 15 – 17 Feb 2006, pp 405-410.

A. Luukanen, P. Helistö, J. S. Penttilä, H. Seppä, H. Sipola, C. R. Dietlein, and E. N. Grossman, "An array of superconducting antenna-coupled microbolometers for passive video-rate THz imaging," Proceedings of Fourth ESA Workshop on Mmw technology and applications, , NL, 15 – 17 Feb 2006, pp 417-422.

FORENSIC SCIENCES

Technical Contact:
Susan Ballou

Staff-Years:
17

The term "forensic" conjures up a vivid association with several major television shows. These shows provide a brief look into the basic principles and theories of forensic sciences and how the sciences are used to solve criminal and civil cases. Although these T.V. shows imply the investigators commonly are experts in all facets of the scientific disciplines, the reality is, that premise is far from the truth. Scientific research at NIST starts with understanding the fundamentals of science, from which standards are created. These standards are the focal point of the forensic science program at the Office of Law Enforcement Standards (OLES). This supporting research may require several months or several years to come to fruition. Whatever the length of time, the end result is a standard that provides the necessary basis by which forensic analysts provide the scientific results that meet judicial acceptability.

The diversity of forensic applications requires a multi-disciplinary approach, and thus work in this area has been distributed across many NIST laboratories. For example, projects relating to computer usage in crimes are based in the Information Technology Laboratory (ITL). These projects address issues such as: the evaluation of investigative software, the prevention of inadvertent modifications of electronic files under investigation and the development of a National Software Reference Library (NSRL) that helps computer analysts to quickly identify suspect files on a hard drive. The Chemical Science and Technology Laboratory (CSTL) has been assigned all aspects of DNA research and the creation of biological standard reference materials (SRMs). The Precision Engineering Division has been assigned projects addressing bullet and cartridge cases and the Building and Fire Research Laboratory (BFRL) handles projects related to burn pattern recognition, measurement and simulation of ignition sources, and computer simulations of actual fire events.

The following text highlights a few of the active projects targeting the needs of the forensic analyst.

PROJECT: COMPUTER FORENSIC REFERENCE DATA SETS (CFReDS)

GOALS

To provide a readily accessible Internet site that can be used by computer forensic analysts and management to obtain mock case examples for in-house evaluation. These case examples can be used to test examiners skills as part of accreditation requirements or to evaluate/calibrate equipment prior to use.

CUSTOMER NEEDS

The burgeoning number of crimes committed with the aid of the computer is overwhelming the nation's crime laboratories. To assist with the "controls" and evaluation of analyst's expertise, management desires a quick and assured method for evaluation. In general, they need test sets that have been validated and are freely available for use to determine the functionality of equipment as well as the skill set of an analyst.

TECHNICAL STRATEGY

The project participants will continue to converse with individuals knowledgeable in the field to determine the type of test sets needed and in what format. The received suggestions will then be evaluated, verified, and if necessary, used to create an appropriate story line. This includes determining what features to include in the data sets, such as; target strings in files, slack space, unallocated space, file system metadata. The tests will be available through the web site, easily accessible by any individual seeking this type of assistance.

DELIVERABLES

- Active web site; http://www.cfreds.nist.gov

PROJECT: COMPUTER FORENSICS TOOLS TESTING (CFTT)

GOALS

To verify the operation and output of software and hardware that is used to examine digital evidence and to provide documentation on the findings for use in judicial proceedings.

Customer Needs

Computer forensic investigators and analysts require documented evaluation of currently available software/hardware (tools) that advertise forensic capabilities. This step is essential to support collection, examination, analysis, and court testimony of digital evidence. NIST is highly suited to provide an unbiased determination of a tool's capability and therefore to verify the results produced by these tools. NIST was asked to provide expertise in developing test suites and a testing framework to structure the testing of the products in use. The information provided by NIST as a neutral party is used to determine several factors: whether specific tools should be used in forensic examinations; how the tools should be used; and the limitations of the tools' capabilities.

Technical Strategy

To assist the computer forensic community NIST has conducted functionality tests on specific software and hardware products. The selection of a specific software/hardware product and its functionality (*e.g.*, imaging) is accomplished through specific listserv announcements and input from select federal agencies. The actual test results are provided in a report form and posted on two different Web sites: http://www.cftt.nist.gov and http://www.ojp.usdoj.gov/nij/sciencetech/welcome.html.

Deliverables

- Published documents describing the overall concept and framework for testing computer forensics tools. Details for the Law Enforcement agency on how to use this information is also provided. Electronic documentation can be found at: http://www.cftt.nist.gov.

Project: DNA Related Projects

Goals

To provide technical support to state and local forensic DNA laboratories regarding the underlying science of available DNA products and STR-based research. To conduct direct instructional support to state and local forensic DNA laboratories through workshops, training sessions and presentations and through continued population of the NIST STRbase web site.

Customer Needs

State and local forensic DNA analysts do not have the time or the funds to conduct research into new technologies or evaluate newly released products. In addition, the incorporation of non-evaluated products into a laboratory's standard protocol requires that laboratory to conduct a lengthy validation. To advance the state-of-the-art and alleviate associated time and cost constraints, NIST undertakes the necessary research, development and evaluation tasks.

Technical Strategy

NIST provides ready access to reference material, new technology and tutorials through a service called strbase, which can be found at http://www.cstl.nist.gov/biotech/strbase/NISTpub.htm. Through this service analysts have resources at their fingertips.

NIST will continue research in such areas as: analysis of degraded DNA through the use of miniSTRs, continue evaluating the applicability of Y-chromosome analysis through the use of Y-SNP markers and Y-STR markers and evaluate and improve tools that will aid state and local crime laboratories in the areas of quality assurance and quality control software, equipment upgrades and variant allele cataloging and characterization.

Deliverables

- To continue to provide service to all state and local DNA laboratories through SRM production, presentations, publications, Web site postings, NIST developed software (*i.e.*, AutoDimer, mixSTR, Multiplex_QA) and release of new technologies.

Project: Ion Mobility Spectrometry (IMS) Trace Drug Detection Devices

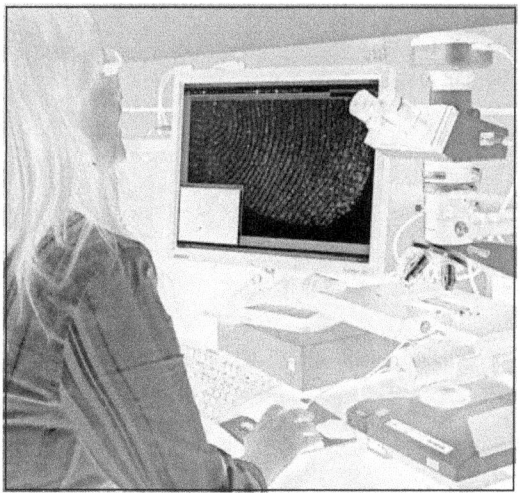

Selecting particles for IMS analysis.

Goals

To research the utilization of the IMS method as applied to contraband drugs to characterize detection efficiency and to develop methods to characterize and standardize swipe-based and portal-based collection efficiencies of contraband drug particles.

Customer Needs

Detection of contraband drugs is a high priority for a large number of law enforcement organizations. A promising technology for screening for trace amounts of contraband drugs is Ion Mobility Spectrometry (IMS), which is also used nationally for the detection of traces of explosives at airports and other points of entry. However, there exists a number of deficiencies, including high false positive alarm rates for some drugs and high false negative rates (lack of detection) for other drugs. Agencies require a general understanding of detection limits, reliability, and false alarm rates for IMS-based systems.

Technical Strategy

To study an immunoassay instrument marketed for law enforcement applications that should have a similar sensitivity to IMS, but better selectivity. In addition, to study a IMS-based portal detector, and two new desktop IMS instruments. This will require the design of a multivariate experiment that includes at least two desktop instruments and tests for a number of factors including temperature, humidity, sample preparation, and sample matrix. Solid phase microextraction (SPME) used in conjunction with IMS will also be studied. The SPME-IMS approach has the potential to provide a faster, easier, and more portable method of drug analysis in biological samples than those commonly used today.

Deliverables

- Test instrument response using desktop IMS instruments. Submit Report of Analysis.
- Evaluate use of PLM/FT-IR spectrometer system for analysis of ngerprints.
- Complete study of effect on false positive rates from common contaminants, adulterants, and excipients.

Project: National Software Reference Library (NSRL)

Goals

To provide several library attributes; a collection of actual commercial-off-the-shelf (cots) software products and a validated database of known software, file profiles, and fe signatures ("fingerprints") in different hash formats.

Customer Needs

The computer forensic analyst is confronted with the examination of an increasing expanse of files per hard drive and in many instances numerous hard drives per forensic case. In addition, all methods and tools utilized in an examination must meet stringent accreditation and judicial requirements.

Technical Strategy

To support the computer forensic investigator or analyst, a validated automated filter program has been created that will either assist in the elimination of thousands of legal files that have no intrinsic forensic value, or provide a quick identification of a specific file of interest. This capability can significantly reduce the amount of examination time required on behalf of the analyst.

Legal requirements may also dictate that the computer forensic analyst produce the basis for the hash values used in an examination, or the specific software version used to obtain the hash. To meet this, NIST retains the actual commercial product that was tested in an in-house library.

Deliverables

- The master database is the primary deliverable (see http://www.nsrl.nist.gov for further information).

- An extracted database that is available to users in CD format. The CD can be purchased through the NIST SRD Office on a subscription basis.

- The compilation of the commercial product library.

PROJECT: STANDARD CASING REFERENCE MATERIAL

GOALS

To provide virtual signature standards and NIST Standard Reference Materials (SRMs) standards for casings to be used with equipment that captures images for comparison purposes.

CUSTOMER NEEDS

Firearm analysts currently utilize in-house standards for equipment calibration and inter-laboratory evaluation. Laboratory accreditation requirements and federal mandates are dictating the use of traceable reference materials in an effort to establish measurement uniformity.

TECHNICAL STRATEGY

Utilizing an electroforming process on casings from actual test fires, a set of master casings has been produced. For maximum signature reproducibility, the decay factor for these masters will be determined. Each casing produced will be evaluated through topography measurements to ensure maximum cross correlation factor (CCF).

DELIVERABLES

- Standard Reference Material (SRM), standard casing.
- Report stating the CCF for all casings produced.

PROJECT: REAL TIME FORENSICS IMAGING FOR ANALOG AND DIGITAL VIDEO TAPES

GOALS

To provide forensic analysts with state-of-the-art, nano-engineered magnetic imaging methods for screening data and recovering data from media that is damaged or was tampered with. This will greatly increase the accuracy of criminal investigations through identification of specific types of machines used, whether or not the tapes are original, and to allow investigators to recover data from catastrophic events.

CUSTOMER NEEDS

Law Enforcement and criminal investigators require to "see" signs of tampering in analog audio tapes – erasing, overdubbing and other alterations – while listening to the tapes. It is also important that law enforcement has systems that can evaluate the authenticity of both analog and digital videotape as well as audio recordings. Because magnetic data storage tape is ubiquitous in surveillance and monitoring devices, it is expected that it will remain a challenge to law enforcement forensics teams. The sheer amount of tape (miles on a single roll) and the high density (down track resolution higher than 0.1 micrometer) renders existing techniques, based on magnetic fluids, obsolete. Real-time magnetic scanners will solve this problem.

TECHNICAL STRATEGY

To develop a high resolution (1600 pixels/inch) imaging system that operates in real-time. This allows investigators to see signs of tampering in analog audiotapes — erasing, overdubbing and other alterations — while listening to the tapes. In FY04-05 we fabricated three complete systems. One of these systems is built around an audiocassette system, and will be deployed at the FBI Audio Laboratory in Quantico, Virginia. The other two systems are modular, and can be connected to a cassette deck, a VHS video player, or a DAT (digital audio tape) player. The two modular systems will be kept at NIST and used for testing and characterizing the sensor arrays and validating this technology for use and presentation in court cases. In addition, for the LOC, NTSB, and NARA it is necessary to explore the efficacy of these systems for both routine and emergency data recovery from damaged and aged magnetic data storage tape media.

In order for this technique to have an impact, it is necessary to do blind and double blind testing of altered and original tapes. These tests will be conducted in close collaboration with the FBI. Validation work in this study will focus on the videotape area.

DELIVERABLES

- Forensics – Complete validation report for the VHS & DAT tape.
- Data recovery – Reel-to-Reel tape, test up to 10 kHz
- Data recovery – Reel-to-Reel tape, test up to 10 kHz

PROJECT: REFRACTIVE INDEX GLASS STANDARD REFERENCE MATERIAL

GOALS

To replenish the depleted NIST standard reference material stock, which is utilized by forensic laboratories that conduct glass analysis.

CUSTOMER NEEDS

To meet quality assurance and accreditation requirements, traceable reference materials must be used when analyzing forensic evidence. The depletion of the NIST glass refractive index standard reference material (SRM) caused some laboratories to seek other options to meet accreditation requirements. Therefore, the forensic community needs a new glass refractive index SRM.

TECHNICAL STRATEGY

Glass samples have been specially annealed to remove residual stress birefringence to ensure uniform optical quality. 5-decimal place index of refraction values will be extracted from the measurements and glass prism samples (7 in total) will be subjected to index of refraction measurements. This portion of the process has been completed. The remaining aspect in the process is density measurement determination.

DELIVERABLES

- A glass standard reference material available for purchase, which, when completed, can be found at https://srmors.nist.gov or http://ts.nist.gov/ts/htdocs/230/232/232.htm.

ACCOMPLISHMENTS

■ National Software Reference Library: Reference Data Set (RDS) is continually upgraded and available at; http://www.nsrl.nist.gov

■ Issued the following Standard Reference Materials (SRMs):

SRM 1828b Ethanol-Water Solutions: Blood-Alcohol Testing: Six Levels

SRM 1847 Ethanol-Water Solutions: Breath-Alcohol Testing: Three levels

SRM 2285 Arson Test Mixture in Methylene Chloride

SRM 2391b PCR-Based DNA Profiling Standard

SRM 2392-I Mitochondrial DNA Sequencing (Human HL-60 DNA)

SRM 2395 Human Chromosome DNA Profiling Standard

SRM 2372 Human DNA Quantification Standard

SRM 2390 DNA Profiling Standard for RFLP Testing

SRM 2460 Standard Bullet

SRM 2891 Ethanol-Water Solutions: (nominal 0.02 % by mass)

SRM 2892 Ethanol-Water Solutions: (nominal 0.04 % by mass)

SRM 2893 Ethanol-Water Solutions: (nominal 0.08 % by mass)

SRM 2894 Ethanol-Water Solutions: (nominal 0.1 % by mass)

SRM 2895 Ethanol-Water Solutions: (nominal 0.2 % by mass)

SRM 2896 Ethanol-Water Solutions: (nominal 0.3 % by mass)

SRM 2897 Ethanol-Water Solutions: (nominal 2 % by mass)

SRM 2898 Ethanol-Water Solutions: (nominal 6 % by mass)

SRM 2899 Ethanol-Water Solutions: (nominal 25 % by mass)

SRM 8107 Additives in Smokeless Gunpowder.

PUBLICATIONS

Duewer, D.L. and Butler, J.M. (2006) MULTIPLEX_QA: an exploratory quality assessment tool for multiplexed electrophoretic assays, *Electrophoresis* (*in press*). [preprint]

Hill, C.R., Butler, J.M., Coble, M.D. (2006) Allele frequencies for 27 new miniSTR loci with U.S. Caucasian, African American, and Hispanic populations. *J. Forensic Sci.* (in press).

Butler, J.M. (2005) Constructing STR multiplex assays. Methods in Molecular Biology: Forensic DNA Typing Protocols (Carracedo, A., ed.), Humana Press: Totowa, New Jersey, 297: 53-66. [preprint].

J. Song, T. Vorburger, T. Renegar, H. Rhee1, A. Zheng, L. Ma, J. Libert, S. Ballou, B. Bachrach and K. Bogart, "Correlation of Topography Measurements of NIST SRM 2460 Standard Bullets by Four Techniques," Meas. Sci. Technology, Jan. 31, 2006.

Test Results for Hardware Write Block Device: FastBloc IDE (Firmware Version 16), NCJ 212956, April 2006, Special Report, National Institute of Justice.

Test Results for Hardware Write Block Device: Digital Intelligence Firefly 800 IDE (FireWire Interface), NCJ 212957, April 2006, Special Report, National Institute of Justice.

Test Results for Hardware Write Block Device: MyKey NoWrite (Firmware Version 1.05), NCJ 212958, April 2006, Special Report, National Institute of Justice.

Test Results for Hardware Write Block Device: ICS Image-Masster DriveLock IDE (Firmware Version 17), NCJ 212959, April 2006, Special Report, National Institute of Justice.

Test Results for Hardware Write Block Device: WiebeTech FireWire DriveDock Combo (FireWire Interface), NCJ 212960, April 2006, Special Report, National Institute of Justice.

Test Results for Hardware Write Block Device: Digital Intelligence UltraBlock SATA (USB Interface), NCJ 212961, April 2006, Special Report, National Institute of Justice.

Test Results for Hardware Write Block Device: WiebeTech Forensic ComboDock (USB Interface), NCJ 214065, May 2006, Special Report, National Institute of Justice.

Test Results for Hardware Write Block Device: Digital Intelligence UltraBlock SATA (FireWire Interface), NCJ 214067, May 2006, Special Report, National Institute of Justice.

Test Results for Hardware Write Block Device: WiebeTech Bus Powered Forensic ComboDock (FireWire Interface), NCJ 214064, May 2006, Special Report, National Institute of Justice.

Test Results for Hardware Write Block Device: WiebeTech Bus Powered Forensic ComboDock (USB Interface), NCJ 214065, May 2006, Special Report, National Institute of Justice.

Test Results for Hardware Write Block Device: WiebeTech Forensic ComboDock (FireWire Interface), NCJ 214066, May 2006, Special Report, National Institute of Justice.

Coble, M.D., Vallone, P.M., Just, R.S., Diegoli, T.M., Smith, B.C., Parsons, T.J. (2006) Effective strategies for forensic analysis in the mitochondrial DNA coding region. Int. J. Legal. Med. 120:27-32. [Supplementary Data].

Butler, J.M., Decker, A.E., Vallone, P.M., Kline, M.C. (2006) Allele frequencies for 27 Y-STR loci with U.S. Caucasian, African American, and Hispanic samples. Forensic Sci. Int. 156:250-260.

Butler, J.M. (2006) Genetics and genomics of core STR loci used in human identity testing. J. Forensic Sci. 51(2): 253-265.

Butler, J.M., Coble, M.D., Decker, A.E., Duewer, D.L., Hill, C.R., Kline, M.C., Redman, J.W., Vallone, P.M. (2006) Setting standards and developing technology to aid the human identity testing community. Progress in Forensic Genetics 11, Elsevier Science: Amsterdam, The Netherlands, International Congress Series 1288, 628-635.

Test Results for Software Write Block Tools: PDBLOCK Version 1.02 (PDF-LITE), NCJ 209831, June 2005, Special Report, National Institute of Justice

Test Results for Software Write Block Tools: PDBLOCK Version 2.00, NCJ 209832, June 2005, Special Report, National Institute of Justice

Test Results for Software Write Block Tools: PDBLOCK Version 2.01, NCJ 209833, June 2005, Special Report, National Institute of Justice

Vallone, P.M., Fahr, K., Kostrzewa, M. (2005) Genotyping SNPs using a UV photocleavable oligonucleotide in MALDI-TOF MS. Methods in Molecular Biology: Forensic DNA Typing Protocols (Carracedo, A., ed.), Humana Press: Totowa, New Jersey, 297: 169-178.

Vallone, P.M., Decker, A.E., Butler, J.M. (2005) Allele frequencies for 70 autosomal SNP loci with U.S. Caucasian, African American, and Hispanic samples. *Forensic Sci. Int.* 149: 279-286.

Kline, M.C., Vallone, P.M., Redman, J.W., Duewer, D.L., Calloway, C.D., Butler, J.M. (2005) Mitochondrial DNA typing screens with control region and coding region SNPs. *J. Forensic Sci.* 50: 377-385.

Kline, M.C., Duewer, D.L., Redman, J.W., Butler, J.M. (2005) Results from the NIST 2004 DNA Quantitation Study. *J. Forensic Sci.*, 50(3): 571-578.

Butler, J.M., Appleby, J.E., Duewer, D.L. (2005) Locus-specific brackets for reliable typing of Y-chromosome short tandem repeat markers. *Electrophoresis* 26: 2583-2590.

Butler, J.M., Decker, A.E., Kline, M.C., Vallone, P.M. (2005) Chromosomal duplications along the Y-chromosome and their potential impact on Y-STR interpretation. *J. Forensic Sci.* 50(4): 853-859.

Kline, M.C., Vallone, P.M., Decker, A.E., Redman, J.W., Duewer, D.L., Butler, J.M. (2005) Testing candidate DNA quantitation standards with several real-time quantitative PCR methods. Proceedings of the 16th International Symposium on Human Identification. http://www.promega.com/geneticidproc/ussymp16proc/abstracts/kline.pdf.

J. Song, E. Whitenton, L. Ma, T. Vorburger and A. Zheng, "Initial Measurement Results for 40 NIST SRM 2460 Standard Bullets," *Proceedings of 2004 MSC (Measurement Science Conference)*, January 15-16, 2004, CA.

Test Results for Disk Imaging Tools: dd Provided with FreeBSD 4.4, NCJ 203095, January 2004, Special Report, National Institute of Justice.

Test Results for Software Write Block Tools: RCMP HDL Vol. 8, NCJ 203196, February 2004, Special Report, National Institute of Justice.

Forensic Examination of Digital Evidence: A Guide for Law Enforcement, NCJ 199408, April 2004, Special Report, National Institute of Justice.

L. Ma, J. Song, E. Whitenton, A. Zheng, T. Vorburger and J. Zhou, "NIST Bullet Signature Measurement System for SRM (Standard Reference Material) 2460 Standard Bullets," *Journal of Forensic Science* Vol. 49, No. 4, July 2004, pp. 649-659.

Test Results for Software Write Block Tools: RCMP HDL Vol. 4, NCJ 206231, August 2004, Special Report, National Institute of Justice.

Test Results for Software Write Block Tools: RCMP HDL Vol. 5, NCJ 206232, August 2004, Special Report, National Institute of Justice.

Test Results for Software Write Block Tools: RCMP HDL Vol. 7, NCJ 206233, August 2004, Special Report, National Institute of Justice.

J. M. Butler, and P. M. Vallone, (2004) High-throughput genetic analysis through multiplexed PCR and multicapillary electrophoresis. *PCR Technologies: Current Innovations (2nd edition)* Weissensteiner, T., Griffin, H.G., Griffin, A. (Eds.) CRC Press: Boca Raton, Chapter 11, pp. 111-120.

R. Schoske, P. M. Vallone, M. C. Kline, J. W. Redman, J. M. Butler (2004) High-throughput Y-STR typing of U.S. populations with 27 regions of the Y chromosome using two multiplex PCR assays, *Forensic Science International* Vol. 139, pp. 107-121.

P. M. Vallone and J. M. Butler, (2004) Multiplexed assays for evaluation of Y-SNP markers in U.S. populations. Progress in Forensic Genetics 10, Elsevier Science: Amsterdam, The Netherlands, *International Congress Series* 1261, pp. 85-87.

J. M. Butler and R. Schoske, (2004) Forensic value of the multicopy Y-STR marker DYS464. Progress in Forensic Genetics 10, Elsevier Science: Amsterdam, The Netherlands, *International Congress Series* 1261, pp. 278-280.

J. M. Butler, E. Buel, F. Crivellente, B. R. McCord, (2004) Forensic DNA typing by capillary electrophoresis: using the ABI Prism 310 and 3100 Genetic Analyzers for STR analysis. *Electrophoresis* Vol. 25, pp. 1397-1412.

P. M. Vallone, R.S. Just, M. D. Coble, J. M. Butler, T. J. Parsons, (2004) A multiplex allele-specific primer extension assay for forensically informative SNPs distributed throughout the mitochondrial genome. *Int. J. Legal Med.*, Vol. 118, pp. 147-157.

J. M. Butler and R. Schoske, (2004) Duplication of DYS19 flanking regions in other parts of the Y chromosome. *Int. J. Legal Med.*, Vol. 118, pp. 178-183.

P. M. Vallone and J. M. Butler, (2004) Y-SNP typing of U.S. African American and Caucasian samples using allele-specific hybridization and primer extension. *J. Forensic Sci.* Vol. 49 (No. 4), pp. 723-732.

D. T. Chung, J. Drabek, K. L. Opel, J. M. Butler, B. R. McCord, (2004) A study on the effects of degradation and template concentration on the efficiency of the STR miniplex primer sets. *J. Forensic Sci.* Vol. 49 (No. 4), pp. 733-740.

J. Drabek, D. T. Chung, J. M. Butler, B. R. McCord, (2004) Concordance study between miniplex STR assays and a commercial STR typing kit, *J. Forensic Sci.* Vol. 49(4), pp. 859-860.

P. M. Vallone and J. M. Butler, (2004) AutoDimer: a screening tool for primer-dimer and hairpin structures. *Biotechniques* Vol. 37(2), pp. 226-231.

P. M. Vallone, A. E. Decker, J. M. Butler, (2004) Allele frequencies for 70 autosomal SNP loci with U.S. Caucasian, African American, and Hispanic Samples., *Forensic Sci. Int., in press*

J. M. Butler, (2004) Short tandem repeat analysis for human identity testing. Current Protocols in Human Genetics, John Wiley & Sons, Hoboken, NJ, Unit 14.8, (*Supplement 41*), pp. 14.8.1-14.8.22.

J. M. Butler, (2004) Constructing STR multiplex assays. Methods in Molecular Biology: Forensic DNA Typing Protocols (Carracedo, A., ed.), Humana Press: Totowa, New Jersey, *in press*

P. M. Vallone, K. Fahr, M. Kostrzewa, (2004) Genotyping SNPs using a UV photocleavable oligonucleotide in MALDI-TOF MS. Methods in Molecular Biology: Forensic DNA Typing Protocols (Carracedo, A., ed.), Humana Press: Totowa, New Jersey, *in press*

M. D. Coble and J. M. Butler, J. M. (2004) Characterization of new miniSTR loci to aid analysis of degraded DNA., *J. Forensic Sci., in press*

D. L. Duewer, M. C. Kline, J. W. Redman, J. M. Butler, (2004) NIST Mixed Stain Study #3: signal intensity balance in commercial short tandem repeat multiplexes, *Anal. Chem., in press*

M. C. Kline, P. M. Vallone, J. W. Redman, D. L. Duewer, C. D. Calloway, J. M. Butler, (2004) Mitochondrial DNA typing screens with control region and coding region SNPs, *submitted*

M. C. Kline, D. L. Duewer, J. W. Redman, J. M. Butler, (2004) Results from the NIST 2004 DNA Quantitation Study, *submitted*

M. A. Menotti-Raymond, V. A. David, L. A. Wachter, L. A., J. M. Butler, S.J. O'Brien, (2004) An STR forensic typing system for genetic individualization of domestic cat (*Felis catus*) samples, *submitted*

J. M. Butler, A. E. Decker, M. C. Kline, P. M. Vallone, (2004) Chromosomal duplications along the Y-chromosome and their potential impact on Y-STR interpretation, *submitted*

E. Whitenton, C. Johnson, D. Kelley, R. Clary, B. Dutterer, L. Ma, J. Song and T. Vorburger, "Manufacturing and Quality Control of the NIST Standard Reference Material 2460 Standard Bullet," *Proceedings of the 2003 ASPE (American Society for Precision Engineering)*, October 28-31, 2003, Portland, OR, pp. 99-102.

J. Song, L. Ma, E. Whitenton and T. Vorburger, "2D and 3D Surface Texture Comparisons Using Autocorrelation Functions," *Proceedings of the 6th ISMTII (International Symposium on Measurement Technology and Intelligent Instruments)*, November 28-29, 2003, Hong Kong.

PUBLIC SAFETY COMMUNICATION SYSTEMS

Too often in critical situations communications the data exchanges between law enforcement and public safety agencies are hampered by equipment incompatibilities. In large part these incompatibilities are due to a lack of standards to provide a common, nationwide approach to telecommunications and information sharing. The Department of Homeland Security's Wireless Public SAFEty Interoperable COMmunications program (SAFECOM), the umbrella initiative to coordinate all Federal, state, local, and Tribal users to achieve national wireless communications interoperability and the Department of Justice's Community Oriented Policing Services (COPS) have a common goal to resolve these issues by supporting the development and implementation of communications standards that will advance communications interoperability.

The OLES Public Safety Communications Systems program provides technical support to both of these programs. The OLES program, drawing on existing standards as well as critical requirements provided by public safety practitioners, provides insight and direction to IT and wireless standards committees that are developing standards for voice, data, image, and video communications. To meet the short term needs of law enforcement and public safety agencies until such standards are in place, the program also evaluates commercial devices that can provide for interim interoperability.

PROJECT: STANDARDIZATION EFFORTS RELATED TO TELECOMMUNICATION AND INFORMATION TECHNOLOGY INTEROPERABILITY

GOALS

The objective of this program is to support the SAFECOM and COPS Programs by providing engineering support through scientific analysis, standards leadership, and a technical liaison to practitioners to promote the identification, development and validation of standards for communication system products and services that support interoperable communications within the Justice/Public Safety/Homeland Security community. Further, OLES provides technical assessments and evaluations of existing and emerging commercial products and services that may provide interim solutions under various interoperability scenarios.

CUSTOMER NEEDS

With the explosion of telecommunications and information technologies has come a disturbing trend – a lack of interoperability among systems. This problem is particularly acute in the justice/public safety community where product lifecycles are especially long and manufacturer proprietary solutions abound. The problem is evidenced over and over as police and other agencies (fire departments, emergency medical services, etc.) fail to communicate with each other during multi-jurisdictional events (such as the Oklahoma City bombing or the September 11 terrorist incidents). Even in the absence of high-profile local, state, or regional calamities, daily interoperability problems continue to plague justice/public safety agencies nationwide.

The focus of the SAFECOM and COPS programs continues to be the development of robust, open telecommunications standards which promote interoperability amongst public safety-related communications devices and systems. In support of interoperable voice communications standards, OLES continued its focused involvement with Project 25 and the Telecommunications Industry Association (TIA) TR 8 standards committees—especially in the development of key interfaces that will fulfill the promise of seamlessly interconnecting different manufacturers' infrastructures. In 2005, at the request of the P25 Steering Committee, OLES expanded its role in TIA by heading the development of a compliance assessment program designed to ensure that users can procure mission-critical Project 25 equipment with a high level of confidence that the equipment complies with the relevant standards.

TECHNICAL STRATEGY

The current phase of the project can be seen as falling into the following five functional support areas:

PUBLIC SAFETY STATEMENT OF REQUIREMENTS AND ARCHITECTURE FRAMEWORK

OLES continues to work with SAFECOM to further develop the *Public Safety Statement of Requirements (PS SoR) for Communications and Interoperability* This document which was initially released in 2004 is the recognized defition of long term communications requirements for the public safety community. The PS SoR provides a vision

Technical Contact:
Dereck Orr

Staff-Years:
25

of public safety's communications and information sharing needs, defined by the practitioners themselves to meet their functional and operational requirements well into the future. The PS SoR is focused on the functional needs of public safety first responders — Emergency Medical Services (EMS) personnel, fire fighters, and law enforcement officers — to communicate and share information as authorized when it is needed, where it is needed, and in a mode or form that allows the practitioners to use it effectively. The communications mode may be voice, data, image, video, or multimedia that includes multiple forms of information. The original PS SoR release focused on qualitative requirements. Since then extensive research has been conducted using subjective practitioner evaluations to establish baseline quantitative requirements for both audio and video quality. The results of this latest research which provide more detail on technical parameters and values are planned to be released as a second of the PS SoR this fiscal year.

Based on the communications requirements outlined in the Public Safety Statement of Requirements, OLES and SAFECOM began development of the Public Safety Architecture Framework (PSAF). The architecture framework will provide public safety agencies with the necessary tools to compare and integrate legacy communication and information systems and allow them to leverage resources and migrate towards interoperability. The PSAF provides practitioners with a set of tools and a common lexicon for describing the elements of their local communications systems and enables practitioners to compare capabilities and equipment to achieve interoperability between jurisdictions. In addition to assisting the SAFECOM program in identifying needed standards by highlighting compatibility problems at key communications interfaces, the PSAF will also serve as a guide for localities planning for interoperability or technical capability upgrades. The PSAF enables engineers and planners to document their current public safety communication capabilities and analyze their system in relation to other systems. Ultimately, the PSAF will provide public safety with the ability to examine and develop both their operational and communications system capabilities.

With the publication of the PSAF in early 2006, OLES and SAFECOM are moving forward with a trial to demonstrate the utility of architecture framework principles within the public safety community by developing a database driven application which doesn't require enterprise architecture expertise. The first stage of the trial will leverage the Communications Assets Survey and Mapping (CASM) tool developed by DHS's Interoperable Communications Technical Assistance Program. The CASM tool's baseline capabilities, which gather operational data, will be extended to gather more technical details of a communications system. Public safety agencies participating in the trial activity will apply their real world experience to shape and define the tool and ensure it and the underlying architecture framework process are user friendly.

PROJECT 25 KEY INTERFACES STANDARDIZATION ACCELERATION

In early 2005 three Project 25 interfaces were identified as crucial for public safety agencies to purchase and implement both operable and interoperable P25-compliant systems. Those interfaces are listed below and represent where the most effective acceleration of the P25 Standards occurred in the past year and a half. While the initial releases will not fully satisfy all of the users' requirements, they will allow manufacturers to build interoperable equipment possessing the most common, basic features.

- ISSI (Inter-RF Subsystem Interface) – This interface allows public safety agencies to interconnect systems on their wired networks (intranets). The initial ISSI protocol specification was approved by the TR8.19 group on May 31, 2006 as a TIA standard. This specification, also known as "Release 1," supports a limited feature set, *i.e.*, trunked voice operation but no over-the-air rekeying (OTAR) for encryption, and limited roaming of mobile radio users between systems. This standard, TIA-102.BACA, was published by TIA in August, 2006. Compliance specification standards for the ISSI are under active development.

- Fixed/Base Station Subsystem Interface (FSSI): This interface allows an RF site (with base station transmitters and receivers) to interconnect with an RF subsystem – the P25 system administrator and controller. The initial FSSI protocol specification was approved by the TR8.19 group on January 11, 2006 as a TIA standard. This standard, TIA-102.BAHA, was published by TIA in June, 2006. Compliance specification standards for the FSSI are under active development.

- Console Subsystem Interface (CSSI): This interface allows public safety dispatchers and communication center supervisors to interconnect via their consoles with an RF subsystem. Completion of the FSSI, which enables direct basic console control of fixed/base station equipment, and the ISSI now serve as the supporting foundations for more comprehensive CSSI standards currently under development.

PROJECT 25 COMPLIANCE ASSESSMENT PROGRAM

In April 2005, at the request of the Project 25 Steering Committee, OLES, again working on behalf of SAFECOM, began efforts to develop a conformity assessment program for Project 25 equipment, now known as the Project 25 Compliance Assessment Program. Since then OLES has worked with representatives from both user and industry communities to focus the efforts of the program and to develop an initial framework for the assessment program. To these ends the Project 25 Compliance Assessment Working Group (CAWG) was formed under the auspices of the Telecommunications Industry Association (TIA) to consider the processes and procedures necessary to implement a program. A key accomplishment of this group was a memorandum of understanding stipulating the basic assumptions for testing and the means by which test results would be collected and disseminated. That group has established a basic framework for the program and decided upon a first-party testing regimen to back a Supplier's Declarations of Compliance.

At the recommendation of OLES, the Project 25 Compliance Assessment Process and Procedures Task Group was formed by expanding the scope of another committee to encompass all of compliance assessment. OLES representatives drafted and the committee accepted a work plan that prioritized the various conformance and interoperability test procedures—the test procedures that underpin the compliance assessment program. Subsequently, TIA has formed the TR-8.25 Compliance Assessment committee to address an increasing number of compliance assessment related issues.

The initial work of the Compliance Assessment Program focused on the Common Air Interface (CAI), the most mature of the P25 interfaces. Testing of the CAI begins with evaluations of interoperability for both trunked and conventional mode operation and are on track for completion by the end of calendar year 2006. Work is ongoing to update and publish more complete interoperability test procedures, and conformance test procedures for the CAI will follow.

Testing of wireline-based interfaces such as the ISSI poses additional challenges not the least of which is the need for new test equipment and metrology. In response to this challenge OLES representatives authored the ISSI Measurement Methods standards document and have undertaken the development of the DoC ISSI Emulation and Test System (DIETS) which provides a set of tools for testing emerging ISSI technologies. The tool will emulate a P25 Radiofrequency Subsystem (RFSS) and exercise the protocols defined in the ISSI standards. A complete test tool is being developed that will implement all of the ISSI conformance test cases being developed by TIA. In addition, the tool will include a packet capture and visualization tool that will support system analysis and troubleshooting. Future incremental enhancements to DIETS would enable the tool to support ISSI performance testing as well. The DIETS architecture is also capable of supporting conformance and performance testing for the Fixed Station and Console interfaces.

PUBLIC SAFETY BROADBAND DATA STANDARDS EFFORTS

OLES is driving the broadband standardization effort on behalf of public safety. OLES leadership in this area is evidenced by its sponsorship of the Chair for the APIC Broadband Task Group, and its support from the public safety community derives from its commitment to faithfully representing their requirements. The OLES strategy is to conduct extensive simulation work based on real world scenarios taken from the Public Safety Statement of Requirements. In support of this effort OLES sponsors the project leader for the simulation effort and coordinates the efforts of a contractor from Booze Allen Hamilton who performs the simulations in OPNET. The goal is for public safety to be able to quantify their specific spectrum needs and tie these needs directly back to a repeatable simulation effort. To date reports summarizing the findings of simulations of the first three discipline-specific scenarios from the Public Safety Statement of Requirements have been produced. These reports have been accepted by all participants in the APIC Broadband Task Group and have essentially become the working group's de facto findings. With OLES support the Task Group will soon be prepared to select an air interface for use in the 4.9 GHz band. This effort marks the first time that public safety will be standardizing broadband data communications, and as such, will have an enormous impact on the way first responders conduct day-to-day business.

OLES is also instrumental in the Project 34 User Needs Working Group. This is a working group made up of practitioners that determines the user needs and requirements for broadband communications. OLES has participated in writing many of the requirements documents produced by the P34 Working Group, including the latest Statement of Requirements for Incident Area Networking.

Owing to its contributions to public safety broadband data standards, OLES has been requested by both the SAFECOM Advisory Group and the National Public Safety Telecommunications Council to participate in a study of how public safety could better utilize the 700 MHz band for broadband data communications. While this work has just begun, it is expected that the deliverables will dramatically impact public safety's use of this spectrum. In support of this role, OLES sponsors the Co-Chair of NPSTC's newly formed Broadband Interoperability Working Group, which is charged with standardizing public safety's 700 MHz broadband spectrum.

OLES is also advancing the work of Project MESA on behalf of first responders in the United States. Project MESA is a global effort to address public safety communications needs and is a cooperative effort between TIA in the United States and ETSI in Europe. Project MESA aims to develop a worldwide set of specifications for public safety to create a global market for equipment and to promote interoperability at the international level. OLES's strategy in Project MESA has been to sponsor the Chair of the Technical Systems Group who then leverages the Public Safety Statement of Requirements to ensure that US public safety agency communications requirements are adequately represented and addressed.

TECHNOLOGY EVALUATION AND ENGINEERING SUPPORT

OLES continues to evaluate commercial interim interoperability products for their ability to satisfy near term interoperability requirements. The various products are selected for evaluation by the SAFECOM Test and Evaluation Working group, which looks for those products which appear to have the greatest potential over the short and long-term as interim interoperability solutions.

OLES also responds to the immediate needs of the SAFECOM and COPS programs by performing other research and applied engineering activities as requested. These activities may include strategic and tactical planning, system engineering, technical analysis, economic benefit studies, etc. OLES also develops formal documents such as guides or handbooks, presentations, white papers, and other documentation to support existing program tasks and/or proposed initiatives. On occasion, at the request of NIJ, OLES provides technical representatives to evaluate proposals, designs, approaches, and other technical overtures submitted/offered to NIJ.

DELIVERABLES

- Revised Statements of Requirements (SORs) for both IT and wireless telecommunications applications, architectural framework documents, NIJ standards, reports, guides, guidelines, handbooks, white papers, and other products required to advance the CommTech Program and other interoperability-related efforts within NIJ.

ACCOMPLISHMENTS

■ OLES representatives hold the following leadership positions in Project 25 related task groups/committees or other organizations:

- Vice-Chair of the ISSI Task Group

- Vice-Chair of the P25 Systems Architecture Working Group (PSAWG)

- Vice-Chair of the Vocoder Task Group

- Vice-Chair of the Compliance Assessment Process and Procedures Task Group

- Chair of the APCO 25 Interface Committee Broadband Task Group

- Vice-Chair of the Technology Committee in the National Public Safety Communications Working Group

- Co-Chair of the Broadband Interoperability Working Group in NPSTC

- Chair of the Security Working Group in NPSTC

- Chair of the VoIP Working Group in NPSTC

- Chair of the Technical Systems Group in Project MESA

■ Provided technical support for SAFECOM's first Voice over IP (VoIP) Industry Roundtable to address the growing problem of the increasing number of incompatible IP-based interoperability gateways. Representatives from public safety VoIP vendors such as Motorola, EADS, MACOM, Twisted Pair, Cisco, Catalyst and public safety representatives from APCO, IACP, FPS were in attendance. A key outcome of this event was a commitment to consider leveraging the efforts of Project 25 ISSI for use as the base set of standards for public safety related VoIP devices.

- Completed a LabVIEW based software test suite to perform automated Radio Performance Measurements on Project 25 Land Mobile Radios. This software will support uniform and repeatable tests of Project 25 subscriber unit performance.

- Demonstrated a functioning prototype of the DoC ISSI Emulation and Test System (DIETS), a SIP-based Project 25 Radiofrequency Subsystem (RFSS) emulator.

- Developed technical approaches and contributions to Project 25 and Project MESA that advanced the definition of user requirements and critical interface standards.

- Assisted COPS and SAFECOM management by developing the technical strategy for formally achieving telecommunications interoperability, deriving the process and procedures for involving local, state, and federal public safety practitioners in the strategy, and creating position papers and outreach documents that will help high-level Government officials better understand the methodology.

- Played key roles in developing and shepherding through approval two critical standards in TIA TR-8: the ISSI (Inter-RF Subsystem Interface) – and the Fixed/Base Station Subsystem Interface (FSSI):

PUBLICATIONS

The following documents provide significant input to the standardization of telecommunications interoperability for the public safety community:

Public Safety Statement of Requirements for Communications and Interoperability Version 1,1, April 2006 DHS/SAFECOM and NIST/OLES (see http://www.safecomprogram.gov).

Public Safety Statement of Requirements for Communications and Interoperability Volume I, Version 1.2 and Volume II, Version 1,0, due to be released this calendar year DHS/SAFECOM and NIST/OLES

Public Safety Architecture Framework Volumes I and Version 1.0, February 10, 2006, DHS/SAFECOM and NIST/OLES (see http://www.safecomprogram.gov).

CBRNE Standards

Critical Incident Technologies

Technical Contacts:
Philip Mattson
Pamela Gray
James Stewart

Staff-Years:
40

Public Safety and Security Technologies

Technical Contacts:
Alim Fatah
Lisa Rothwell

Staff-Years:
12

Long before September 11, 2001, OLES was heavily engaged in domestic preparedness and homeland security, particularly in developing performance standards for countermeasures against chemical, biological, radiological, nuclear, and explosive (CBRNE) agents. The first OLES CBRNE programs centered on developing CBRNE protective equipment for the emergency response community and were initially funded by the National Institute of Justice (NIJ) beginning in 1999. These programs continue today and form the core of a greatly expanded OLES effort. In FY2003 primary funding of OLES's CBRNE programs shifted from NIJ to the Office for Domestic Preparedness, Grants and Training (G&T) and in 2004 shifted again, to the Science and Technology (S&T) Directorate of the Department of Homeland Security (DHS).

Shared Management Responsibilities

OLES's steadily growing role in CBRNE standards development has required a number of organizational changes. Prior to 2001, OLES's protective equipment projects were managed by its Chemical Systems and Materials Program. As the number and diversity of CBRNE projects grew, however, OLES recognized the need to consolidate its ongoing projects and new projects under a single administrative banner. And so, in 2001, OLES created its **Critical Incident Technologies (CIT)** program area. CIT expanded significantly in FY2003 and FY2004, and matured further through FY2005 and FY2006, overseeing a broad range of standards development activities in many divergent areas. This growth necessitated further changes to ensure adequate management, and in 2005 OLES redefined its Chemical Systems and Materials program area to assume management of specific types of CBRNE programs, and renamed it the **Public Safety and Security Technologies (PSST)** program.

Today, CIT and PSST share management of OLES's portfolio of CBRNE-related programs. CIT is responsible for standards-development projects related to personal protective equipment (PPE); emergency response operational equipment, such as urban search and rescue (US&R) robots; border and transportation security; cybersecurity; and infrastructure protection. PSST manages standards-development projects focusing on CB and explosives detection, CB decontamination, riot control PPE, and less-than-lethal chemical technologies, such as pepper spray. PSST also compiles and updates CBRNE equipment guides for emergency responders and conducts programs related to non-intrusive detection of illegal drugs.

Each program area is discussed in a separate section below.

Meeting Customer Requirements

The CIT and PSST program areas address the requirements of America's emergency response and homeland security communities for integrated suites of performance standards, supporting test protocols, appropriate conformity assessment programs, and user guidance related to equipment and practices. These needs are broadly described in documents such as the Homeland Security Presidential Directives, National Security Presidential Directives, and the National Plan for Homeland Security.

The programs also fulfill the requirements of specific customers within the broader public safety and security community, such as emergency responders (law enforcement, fire service, medical, HAZMAT, and others), the U.S. Coast Guard, U.S. Customs and Border Protection, the U.S. Secret Service, operators of key infrastructure (water, power, transportation), and the information community. Typically, specific customer needs are identified through studies, surveys, working groups, professional and trade associations, and similar avenues, such as NIJ's Law Enforcement and Corrections Technology Advisory Council (LECTAC). The InterAgency Board for Equipment Standardization and InterOperability (IAB) serves an important role in identifying and validating requirements, and OLES serves as the organization's Executive Agent for standards development. Requirements are also identified by monitoring emerging science and technology and their potential applications.

Project Funding and Execution

Both CIT and PSST oversee projects spanning many disciplines. The Department of Homeland Security (DHS) Science and Technology Directorate's Standards Office sponsors most of this work, although the National Institute of Justice (NIJ) and NIST itself also sponsor projects managed by these program areas. The scientific and technical work involved in these projects is conducted at NIST and at other organizations, including the National Institute for Occupational Safety and Health (NIOSH), the U.S. Army Edgewood Chemical Biological Center (ECBC), and the U.S. Army Natick Soldier Center. For the DHS-funded projects, the actual bench work is conducted by other OLES program areas and through the Thrust Area Coordinators identified by DHS S&T, and the CIT and PSST program managers serve as DHS technical contacts.

TECHNICAL STRATEGY

In its over 30 years of developing standards for the criminal justice community, OLES developed a uniform process for developing minimum performance standards for critical equipment, based on its expertise in completing scores of projects on behalf of the criminal justice and public safety communities. The process (see figure below) has proven so effective that OLES and many of OLES's technical partners have adopted it to guide the development of standards not only for CBRNE equipment but also for other types of equipment standards. Some of OLES's standards-development projects require following the entire process; others may be more limited in scope and may not require completion of the whole process illustrated in the figure below.

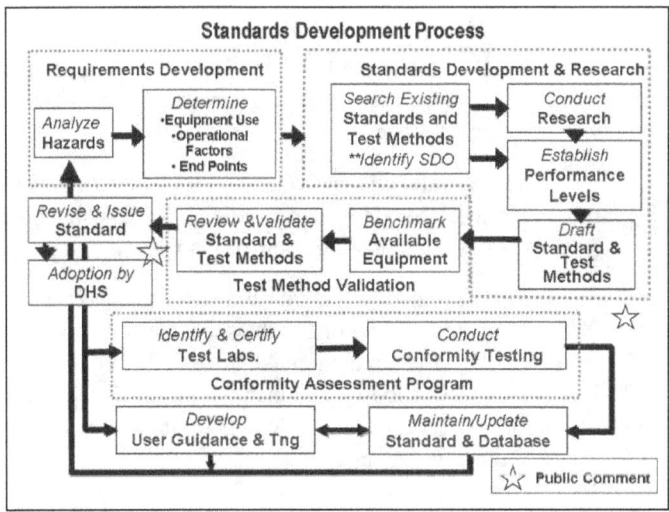

Standards Development Process.

Requirements Development. The first step is to develop the requirements for the standard. A threat and hazard analysis is used to determine the requirements of the user, what the responder needs the equipment to do and under what conditions. In the analysis, a number of factors need to be addressed such as: what is the threat that is to be countered? What is the use of the technology? What environmental conditions need to be considered; *i.e.* temperature, humidity ranges to be considered, flame resistance, etc.? What key endpoints must be measured, *i.e.* is it detection of specific agents and at a what range of concentrations?

Standards Development and Research. The next step is the development of the performance standard and test methods to evaluate the performance of the equipment to the standard. Maximum use is made of the voluntary consensus standards development process, the development and promulgation of the standards through recognized Standards Development Organizations (SDO) such as ASTM International, the American National Standards Institute (ANSI), AOAC International, and other such organizations. A review of existing standards and test methods is conducted to identify: 1) standards and test methods that meet the requirements as identified, or 2) standards and test methods that if modified could meet the requirement, or 3) if no such standards and test methods exist, then identify the appropriate SDO for development and promulgation of the new standard, and initiate the development of the standard through the SDO. In some cases supporting research must be conducted as part of the standards development process to provide technical support in the development of the standard or supporting test methods.

Test Method Validation. Once the draft standard and test methods have been developed, the next step is to procure commercially available products, and test them to the draft standard. This process validates the test methods, in that the test methods can be translated to standard operation procedures that qualified laboratories can use and implement, and it benchmarks currently available equipment. If no equipment benchmarked meets the standard, then the standard must be closely scrutinized. If however, the preliminary benchmarking indicates that no equipment can meet the standard, even with modifications by the manufacturer, then the performance standards and the test methods must be reevaluated. Decisions must be made whether or not to revise the standards and test methods based on the results of the initial benchmark testing without sacrificing health and safety requirements or to maintain the standards as drafted.

Revise and Issue Standard. After identifying all concerns, the standard is issued or promulgated by the appropriate SDO. One key component of this program is the adoption of these standards by the Department of Homeland Security. This ties compliance to appropriate standards with the federal grants programs, in compliance with Homeland Security Presidential Directive (HSPD) & (National Preparedness).

Conformity Assessment Program. The development of performance standards and test methods to evaluate performance to these standards does not ensure that the equipment going to the responders does indeed meet these standards. Programs must be put in place to use the test methods to evaluate conformity to the appropriate standards. The details of these conformity assessment programs will vary, depending on the type of technology being evaluated, the consequence of non-conformance to the standard, whether the standard promulgated by a particular SDO contains provisions for conformity assessment and a number of other factors. Appropriate third party test facilities must be identified that satisfactorily conduct the testing, and the appropriate test management and certification program must be established.

User Guidance and Training. The standards and associated test methods by necessity are very specific and technical documents. The capabilities and limitations on the performance of the technology must be translated in terms that are understandable and useable by the end users of the equipment. They must know whether the system has been tested against Toxic Industrial Chemicals/Materials (TIC/TIMs) or just against Chemical Warfare Agents. Development and distribution of this type of information is essential for the user, the procurement official, and in the development of concepts of operation and training programs. Training programs and concepts of operations (CONOPS) must be adapted or developed to effectively use and understand the capabilities of technologies that meet these standards.

Maintenance of Standard. There must be provisions for the review and update of the standard. As experience is gained in the use of the standard, as new technologies and test methods become available, or in the case of unforeseen problems with the standard and test method, the standard will require periodic revisions. Most SDOs have procedures to accomplish these tasks, and this will be one of the considerations in selecting the appropriate SDO for the development and promulgation of any new standard. A list of compliant equipment must be maintained and available for the user community. One such portal is the DHS-funded Responder Knowledge Base.

Public Comment. This process is not conducted in a vacuum. Public comment from users, developers, manufacturers and other concerned individuals and organizations is critical in the development of the standards. There are a number of points within the process where such comment will be actively solicited.

CRITICAL INCIDENT TECHNOLOGIES (CIT)

GOALS

The primary goals of the CIT Program are to:

1) Develop performance standards, test and evaluation protocols, reference materials and reference data, conformity assessment programs and user guidance for products and services.

2) Develop consistent and verifiable measures of technology effectiveness in terms of basic functionality, reliability, appropriateness and adequacy for the task, interoperability, efficiency, and sustainability.

3) Work with the DHS and DOJ to link equipment compliance with minimum performance standards to grants processes.

4) Provide guidance on technology investments to allow DHS, NIJ, Federal, state, and local stakeholders to optimize use of limited resources.

5) Disseminate standards and subsequent performance evaluations to the sponsors and stakeholders, to help them make informed equipment purchases and to guide manufacturers, developers, and the test and evaluation community to ensure product compliance.

6) Provide guidance to sponsors and stakeholders on cross-cutting standards issues.

CIT PROGRAM AREA PROJECTS

Following are descriptions of three CIT projects.

DHS-FUNDED PROJECTS

CBRNE Countermeasures Thrust Area Projects. These projects focus on standards related to the detection of chemical, radiological and nuclear threats, including standards for existing or new types of sensors and data analysis techniques. Activities aim at developing suites of performance standards, test and evaluation protocols, reference materials and reference data, conformity assessment programs and user guidance for preventing, detecting, responding to, investigating, and recovering from CBRNE incidents.

- **Radiation and Nuclear Standards and Validation.** *Objective*: Develop National Standards for Homeland Security radioactivity, radiation and neutron measurements, and the technical infrastructure to support these standards.

- **National Standards for X-ray and Gamma Ray Security Screening Systems.** *Objective*: Develop consensus standards for X-ray and gamma-ray screening equipment, and measurements to support and validate these standards at NIST.

Borders and Transportation Security Thrust Area Projects. This thrust area focuses on Biometrics, Cargo Security, and Radio Frequency Identification (RFID). Standards for components and systems in border and transportation security are critical to systems for protecting our ports and borders and improving security of our transportation networks.

- **Standards for Rapid Evaluation.** *Objective*: Establish standards for the procedural offline and automated evaluation of biometric data.

- **Latent Fingerprint Analysis.** *Objective*: Develop standardized latent fingerprint identification protocols.

- **Usability for Biometric Systems.** *Objective*: Develop user interface guidelines, a reference user interface, and evaluation methodologies to improve the usability of biometric software systems.

- **Standards for Image Quality.** *Objective*: Develop standard definitions and measurements of finger and face image quality.

- **Multimodal Biometric Accuracy Research Kiosk (MBARK)** · *Objective*: Design, develop, integrate and deploy a standard reference multimodal biometric accuracy research kiosk to collect, maintain and evaluate biometric data.

- **Cargo Security Requirements Denition.** *Objective*: Develop standards for advanced devices and systems to enhance the security of shipping containers and cargo handling processes.

- **Radio Frequency Identification (RFID) Standards.** *Objective*: Develop appropriate functional tests and performance metrics to facilitate reliable use of Radio Frequency Identification (RFID) systems for homeland security and first responder applications.

Preparedness and Response Thrust Area Projects. These projects focus on developing standards that will enable emergency responders to identify and purchase reliable personal protective equipment and operational equipment. The emphasis is on identifying gaps in the existing body of standards and coordinating development of new or modified standards to fill those gaps. The projects range across six areas of concern: Incident Management, Communications, Training, Personal Protective and Operational Equipment (PPOE), Urban Search and Rescue (US&R) Robots, and Geographic Information System (GIS) Standards.

- **Incident Management Standards.** *Objective*: Develop standards in the areas of incident management, preparedness, planning, and training of first responders.

- **Performance Metrics and Standards for RF Equipment.** *Objective*: Provide performance metrics and propagation data to facilitate development of transmission standards for radio-frequency (RF)-based emergency equipment for first responders.

- **NIOSH CBRN Respiratory Standards Development.** *Objective*: Develop performance standards for CBRN respirators

- **ECBC Support to CBRN Respiratory Standards Development.** *Objective*: Facilitate Edgewood Chemical Biological Center (ECBC) technical support to NIOSH's National Personal Protective Technologies Laboratory (NPPTL) and the overall standards development effort. ECBC's support enables the effort to build on research and development conducted within military respiratory programs.

- **Standards Program Development for First Responder Communications.** *Objective*: Develop performance metrics and transmission standards for RF-based emergency equipment.

- **Permeation Through Nonporous Barrier Polymers.** *Objective*: Develop test methods to assess permeation through selective PPE protective materials.

- **Respiratory Threats for First Responders**· *Objective*: Develop performance metrics and testing protocols to support standards development for real time environmental and personal exposure monitoring equipment.

- **Development of Verication Method for Gas Mask Fit Test.** *Objective*: Develop performance metrics and testing protocols to support standards development for selection of appropriate-sized respiratory face masks.

- **Chemical/Biological Personal Protective Equipment Standards.** *Objective*: Develop minimum performance standards and testing methodologies for chemical (both warfare agents and toxic industrial chemicals) and biological protective ensembles for the emergency response community.

- **Emergency Responder Protection Against TICs/TIMs.** *Objective*: Conduct TIC/TIM testing on representative PPE ensemble material to validate testing methodology. Select TICs and TIMs based on the prioritization process previously established.

- **Wear and Tear for Tactical Law Enforcement CB Ensemble.** *Objective*: Assess whether current test methods and protocols available for artificial wear and weathering of materials accurately reflect the use of CB protective ensembles during Homeland Security Operations (HLSO).

- **Reactive Cooling Systems.** *Objective*: Develop performance metrics and standard testing protocols for first responder protective clothing that uses reactive cooling to respond to short duration high thermal load.

- **Microclimate Cooling Systems.** *Objective*: Develop requirements for Microclimate Cooling Systems (MCS) for selected user groups within the DHS/Emergency Response community.

- **Thermal Imager Standards for the Fire Service.** *Objective*: Evaluate the adequacy of current thermal equipment standards for electronic devices used by first responders for location purposes.

- **Personal Alert Safety Systems (PASS Technology).** *Objective* Develop appropriate functional tests and performance metrics to facilitate reliable use of PASS systems for homeland security and first responder applications.

- **Development of Next Generation High Explosives Standards Requirements.** *Objective*: Develop a standard and measurement infrastructure for calibration, standardization, and optimization of trace explosives detection systems.

- **Explosive Containment Standards Development (Blast Resistant Trash Receptacles).** *Objective*: Develop standards and test methods for blast resistant trash receptacles (BRTRs).

- **Bomb Disposal Robot User Interface Standards.** *Objective*: Develop disaster taxonomy and robot performance definitions, as well as operating procedures and user guides.

- **Urban Search and Rescue Robot Metrics & Standards.** *Objective*: Develop comprehensive standards for the development, testing, and certification of technologies for sensing, mobility, navigation, planning, and operator interaction within search and rescue robot systems.

- **Testing and Measurement Methodology for Indoor Localization and a User Guide.** *Objective*: Develop standard and user guide for low rate ultra wideband technology for communication and ranging.

- **Thermal Exposure Measurement Method for First Responders.** *Objective*: Develop test methodologies to determine thermal measurements and calculations of heat buildup and insulation failure in existing protective clothing.

Cyber Security and Critical Infrastructure Protection Thrust Area Projects. Modern buildings and information networks are complex and vulnerable to both external and internal threats. These projects focus on modeling, simulating and analyzing heating, ventilation, and air-conditioning (HVAC) systems and developing standards for building automated controls, integrated sensors, structural integrity, and cyber security countermeasures. The emphasis is on leveraging the rapid technological developments in the private sector and coordinating them with the needs of various DHS components.

- **Standards and Metrics for SCADA and Industrial Control Systems.** *Objective*: Develop standards and software assurance metrics to help SCADA and Industrial Control Systems conform to requirements, standards, and procedures.

- **Economic Standards for Security Related Issues in Constructed Facilities.** *Objective*: Develop a suite of economic standards and an economic training module and software product on how to apply standards to aid in the selection of cost effective strategies for the management of risks associated with terrorism and natural hazards.

- **Standards Development for Gaseous Air Cleaning in Buildings.** *Objective*: Develop standards and test methods for assessing the performance of gaseous air cleaning devices and the level of protection that can be achieved in buildings.

- **Standards and Test Methods for Sensor Networks and Alert Systems.** *Objective*: Develop standards and protocols for sensor interfaces for interoperable links for sensor networks.

- **Personal Identity Verification and Access Control for Buildings.** *Objective*: Develop standards for the integration of building automation systems to address the requirements of personal identity and access control systems.

- **Next Generation Design Economics for Structural Integrity.** *Objective*: Develop technical basis for structural and economics standards that enable users to select cost effective engineering solutions when designing new building or upgrading existing structures to resist progressive structural collapse.

- **Authentication Effectiveness Metrics.** *Objective*: Develop metrics and protocols for assessing the effectiveness of various authentication mechanisms for local and remote environments.

- **Universal Access Control Mechanism.** *Objective*: Develop a standard access control that can meet the diverse access control needs of government and industry.

- **Building Secure Configurations/ Security Settings/Security Checklists.** *Objective*: Develop standards for the integration of building automation systems to address the requirements of personal identity and access control systems.

DHS Office of Interoperability and Compatibility Project. The Office of Interoperability and Compatibility (OIC) has funded the IAB to establish a new Compatibility and Interoperability Committee to examine, identify and report on interoperability and compatibility issues.

NIJ-Funded Projects

Development of Bomb Disposal Robot Standards. *Objective*: Develop equipment standards and test methods based on defined operational requirements.

Development of Bomb Suit Standard. *Objective*: Develop standards and test metrics to assess the operational capability of PPE based on defined operational requirements.

OLES-Funded Projects

Structural Collapse Prediction. *Objective*: Develop risk assessment protocols to assist in the evaluation of structures to endure specific risks related to terrorism and environmental hazards.

Human/Machine Interface Standards for Bomb Disposal Robots. *Objective*: Develop standards and test metrics to evaluate the human/machine interface mechanisms required during specific operational requirements for bomb disposal robots.

DELIVERABLES

- Major deliverables for all of the programs listed above include monthly, quarterly, and annual progress reports, ongoing hazard threat analyses reports, draft and final performance standards, hosting of public hearings on proposed standards, contributions to interagency groups, staffing and equipping a suitable test laboratory, publication of user guides, and other relevant products and reports required to fully implement the standards development activities.

Accomplishments

The Critical Incident Technologies program area was established in 2001 in order to consolidate and adequately manage ongoing and new OLES programs related to public safety and security. Among the milestones achieved to date are:

- Standards for four types of radiation detection equipment were developed and promulgated through IEEE and adopted by the Department of Homeland Security in February 2004. Testing is being conducted at DOE National Laboratories. Five additional standards have been drafted and are in final stages of approval and publication by ANSI. Two rounds of testing have been conducted on commercially available radiation detectors; one has been published, the other is under final editorial review.

- CBRN Self-Contained Breathing Apparatus Standard (SCBA), December 2001. Dozens of different models of respirators from six major manufacturers have been certified to date. Certification testing is ongoing.

- CBRN Air Purifying Respirator Standard, March 2003. Certification testing is ongoing.

- CBRN SCBA retrofit kit approval, March 2003. This allows previously purchased non-CBRN certified respirators to be upgraded to the CBRN standard.

- CBRN APR and Self Contained Escape Mask Standard, October 2003. Certification testing is ongoing.

- CBRN Powered Air Purifying Respirator (PAPR) standard complete, awaiting implementation by NIOSH.

- Adoption of the completed CBRN respirator standards by the Interagency Board for Equipment Standardization and Interoperability, the Office for Domestic Preparedness, and the Department of Homeland Security. In addition, the National Fire

Protection Agency is referencing the NIOSH CBRN respirator standards in the NFPA standards.

- Using simulations developed as a result of user input, the program has determined the appropriate chemical agent concentrations a protective suit must endure in hot and warm zones. Initially this mode was developed using GB and HD, as they are primary agents challenging the respirators. However, additional agents are now being studied as they may pose a greater percutaneous threat.

- NFPA 1991 and 1994 CBR respirator standards have been revised by NFPA to incorporate CW agent concentrations and endpoints.

- To ensure that users of protective CBRN ensembles experience minimal negative health effects and no lasting health effects, the health community performed a health hazard assessment, "Evaluation of Chemical Warfare Agent Percutaneous Vapor Toxicity: Derivation of Toxicity Guidelines for Assessing Chemical Protective Ensembles," July 2003, by Annetta Watson, Dennis Opresko and Veronique Hauschild.

- A draft set of recommendations has been presented to the NFPA for development of a new standard for thermal imagers.

- The PASS project identified a shortcoming in the existing NFPA standard, and a warning was sent to the users through the NFPA, NIOSH and the IAFF. Modifications are being made in the next revision to the standard.

PUBLIC SAFETY AND SECURITY TECHNOLOGIES

The Public Safety and Security Technologies (PSST) program oversees a broad range of standards development activities and coordinates and manages interagency agreements to develop several types of emergency response equipment. PSST-managed projects are executed at NIST and at other organizations, including the U.S. Army Edgewood Chemical Biological Center (ECBC), the Defense Technical Information Center (DTIC), and the Chemical and Biological Information Analysis Center (CBIAC).

GOALS

The primary objectives of the PSST program are to:

1) Develop performance standards, test and evaluation protocols, standard reference materials (SRMs) and reference materials (RMs), reference data, and user guidance for equipment used for detecting of chemical and biological agents and explosives, and for decontamination of chemical and biological agents;

2) Develop CBRNE equipment guides for emergency responders;

3) Develop standards for riot control personal protection equipment (PPE) for law enforcement and corrections officers;

4) Perform technical studies and standards for chemical-based less-than-lethal (LTL) technologies; and

5) Develop non-intrusive technologies and methods used by the criminal justice community for detecting drugs in the human body.

PSST PROGRAM AREA PROJECTS

Following are descriptions of two PSST projects.

CBRNE COUNTERMEASURES THRUST AREA PROJECTS

Projects in this area focus on standards related to CRBNE threat detection, including standards for existing and new types of sensors, data analysis techniques, and decontamination methodologies. Program activities focus on the development of a comprehensive suite of performance standards, test and evaluation protocols, reference materials and reference data and user guidance for the effective prevention, detection, response, recovery and forensic investigation of CBRNE incidents. Projects within this area include:

- **Chemical Standards Program Development.** *Objective* : Coordinate efforts among National Laboratories, Standards Development Organizations, and other professional organizations to assure that first responders have the instrumentation and procedures necessary to make rapid, reliable decisions using field instruments in challenging situations.

- **Development of Chemical Detection Equipment Standards.** *Objective*: Establish appropriate detection levels for toxic industrial chemicals (TICSs) and toxic industrial materials (TIMs), based on the operational performance requirements.

- **Development of Chemical Decontamination Standards.** *Objective*: Determine the level at which a chemical material is no longer considered a health hazard and to which decontamination equipment must neutralize that material.

- **National Independent, Validated Raman Libraries for Forensic and Security Applications.** *Objective*: Develop a validated reference library of Raman spectral signatures of TICs, for use in qualitative identification.

- **Instrumentation and Protocols for First Responder Chemical Detectors.** *Objective*: Define user requirements to ensure that detectors meet the operational requirements of the responder community.

- **Biological Standards Program Development.** *Objective*: Develop a comprehensive suite of performance standards, test and evaluation protocols, reference materials and data, conformity assessment programs, and user guides.

- **Reference Materials for Testing Biothreat Detection Devices and Instruments.** *Objective*: Develop uniform, well-characterized reference materials based on Bacillus anthracis spores and ricin.

- **Development of National Sampling Standards for Suspicious Powders.** *Objective*: Develop a national sampling standard for suspicious powders, to be validated by the AOAC and adopted by ASTM.

- **Development of a Standard and Measurement Infrastructure for Trace Explosive Detection Systems.** *Objective*: Develop the technical tools required to characterize, optimize, calibrate, and standardize trace explosive detection equipment.

- **Trace Particle Explosives Standard Reference Materials.** *Objective*: Develop standard reference materials (SRMs) that provide calibrated trace amounts of high explosives.

- **National Standards for X-ray and Gamma Ray Security Screening Systems.** *Objective*: Develop consensus standards for X-ray and gamma-ray screening equipment, and measurements to support and validate these standards at NIST.

- **Drop on Demand Inkjet Printing of Homeland Security Standards.** *Objective*: To develop inkjet printing technology as a viable method for producing standards to calibrate and validate tabletop, handheld, and portal instruments for the detection of trace explosives, narcotics and chemical warfare agents.

- **Metrology for Integrated Gas Sensors** *Objective*: To promote and support the development of hardware and software standards for specifying embedded-sensor (ES) virtual-components (VCs) for law enforcement and homeland security applications, such as breath analyzers and detectors of toxic gases, trace explosives, and fire accelerants.

To make the ES-VCs compatible with the System-on-a-Chip (SoC) integration methodology used for digital IC design. This NIST effort will enable gas sensor ES-VCs to be included in SoC CAD libraries and enable integration of these ES-VCs with existing digital VCs used ubiquitously by industry to design large ICs.

To deliver working prototype single-chip smart sensor SoCs incorporating ES-VCs, and work with electronic-design-automation (EDA) vendors to make the ES-VCs available in commercial CAD libraries.

- **Standards and Quality Assurance for Biological and Chemical Threat Agents.** *Objective*: To create a program to develop and characterize standard materials and measurement methods to test and improve devices and methods for detecting and identifying chemical and biological agents.

To coordinate related CW and BW standards development efforts within DoD and work being done on TICs and TIMs by EPA, OSHA, and DHS.

- **Detection of Toxins in the Water Supply.** *Objective*: To develop autonomous sensor systems, using a microfluidic platform, for monitoring drinking water for the presence of chemical agents.

- **Test of the Molecular Basis of Virulent Bacteria.** *Objective*: To test the mechanisms by which virulent bacteria kill cells, in support of efforts to develop more timely and effective therapeutic agents.

PROTECTIVE CLOTHING AND EQUIPMENT

Law enforcement, corrections, and security personnel require special personal protective equipment (PPE) when operating in violent situations, in order to protect them from threats such as blunt trauma, slashes, bites, burning petrol, and chemical exposure. Different articles of PPE (helmets, gloves, boots, armor) must not only meet appropriate standards but also be compatible and complementary in order to provide optimum overall protection.

- **Protective Clothing.** *Objective:* To develop a performance standard for PPE for violent situations. With BSI's permission, OLES is undertaking transforming BS 7971 into a U.S. standard and issuing it as an NIJ Standard for use by U.S. law enforcement, corrections, and public safety and security personnel. While retaining the technical content of the British standard, OLES will apply relevant U.S. Safety requirements as promulgated by Occupational Safety and Health Administration (OSHA) and the Code of Federal Regulations (CFR).

DELIVERABLES

- Major deliverables include monthly, quarterly and annual progress reports, ongoing hazard threat analyses reports, draft and nal performance standards, hosting of public hearings on proposed standards, contributions to interagency groups, staf ng and equipping a suitable test laboratory, publication of user guides, and other relevant products and reports required to fully implement the standards development activities.

ACCOMPLISHMENTS

■ Three Decontamination Reports were fialized during FY2004: 1) a report defi ning the quantity of liquid chemical warfare agents that may be deposited on personnel located near a terrorist event, and where on their bodies the deposits are likely to occur; 2) a chemical kinetics study recommending optimum contact times, decontaminate concentration and negative effects of certain contaminate /decontaminate reactions; and 3) a report containing preliminary determination of chemical contamination residuals allowable by the medical community.

■ The trace explosive detection standards project has accomplished a number of milestones, including: 1) publication of NIST IR 7240 "IMS-based Trace Explosives Detectors for First Responders;" 2) a pilot study of deployment of IMS-based explosives detector in partnership with NIST's Physical Security Office; 3) development of solution-based test kits for trace explosive detectors; 4) generation of inkjet printed test materials for a pilot study for trace explosive detectors; 5) construction of a prototype vapor calibrator; 6) submission of ASTM standard practice WK8290; and 7) feasibility studies for the production of particle standards.

■ Almeida, J., Cole, K.D., and Wang, Lili, "Development of Standard Bacillus Spore Suspensions," American Society of Microbiology, Biodefense Meeting Baltimore, MD, March 21, 2005.

■ Workshop on Reference Materials for Biodefense, sponsored by NIST, DoD, and DHS, held at NIST, Gaithersburg, MD, September 13, 2005.

■ Standard for sampling of suspicious powders successfully balloted through ASTM.

■ Work with vendors of test equipment and their customers to determine the type of reference material that will provide the most realistic tests of explosives detection equipment.

■ Ongoing efforts continue on the draft of a chemical vapor detection standard, which includes additional tests and procedures based on user requirements or the interferents study. Input will be provided in accordance with ASTM, or other standards organization timelines. The standard is currently being balloted through ASTM.

■ Submitted draft ASTM standards for air and water heaters used in decontamination operations, and completed explosive test chamber studies to validate CWA hazard analyses.

■ A number of reports have been published on the Raman spectra of agents and chemicals of interest.

■ E2413-04 Standard Guide for Hospital Preparedness and Response is under review for update and coordination with the rewrite of NFPA 473. ASTM Work Item WK5498 has been established to develop a Standard Guide for Developing Model Emergency Operations Plans for All-hazard Events. ASTM Work Item WK5516 has been established to develop a Standard Guide for Building Indoor Dispersion Analysis, Modeling and Health Effect Assessment.

■ Guides that give first responders comprehensive listings of personal protective equipment, chemical and biological detection equipment, chemical and biological decontamination equipment and emergency fi rst responder communication equipment. These guides are published in hard copy format and are available for download from the OLES web site at http://www.eeel.nist.gov/oles/ and on a searchable CD-ROM. Revised second editions of the chemical and biological detector guides have been published. The personal protective equipment guide has been revised and is currently undergoing editorial review. The fi nal guides in the series – explosive and radiation detection equipment – are being drafted.

■ The project to develop a calibration method for the gas mask fi t test has completed the fi rst NIST traceable aerosol concentration measurements. The test method was developed and a technical report and other papers have been published, and the transfer standard has been conferred to the Army.

THE ELECTRONICS AND ELECTRICAL ENGINEERING LABORATORY

One of NIST's seven Measurement and Standards Laboratories, EEEL conducts research, provides measurement services, and helps set standards in support of: the fundamental electronic technologies of semiconductors, magnetics, and superconductors; information and communications technologies, such as fiber optics, photonics, microwaves, electronic displays, and electronics manufacturing supply chain collaboration; forensics and security measurement instrumentation; fundamental and practical physical standards and measurement services for electrical quantities; maintaining the quality and integrity of electrical power systems; and the development of nanoscale and microelectromechanical devices. EEEL provides support to law enforcement, corrections, and criminal justice agencies, including homeland security.

EEEL consists of four programmatic divisions and two matrix-managed offices:

Semiconductor Electronics Division

Optoelectronics Division

Quantum Electrical Metrology Division

Electromagnetics Division

Office of Microelectronics Programs

Office of Law Enforcement Standards

This document describes the technical programs of the Office of Law Enforcement Standards (OLES). Similar documents describing the other Divisions and Offices are available. Contact NIST/EEEL, 100 Bureau Drive, MS 8100, Gaithersburg, MD 20899-8100, Telephone: (301) 975-2220, On the Web: www.eeel.nist.gov

Cover caption: The Office of Law Enforcement Standards (OLES) helps criminal justice, public safety, emergency responder, and homeland security agencies make informed procurement, deployment, applications, operating, and training decisions primarily by developing performance standards, measurement tools, operating procedures, and equipment guidelines. Our logo (top center) reflects some of the projects that we conduct: DNA research, arson research, forensic sciences, and law enforcement weapons and equipment. Shown on the cover are pictures that represent some of the projects in our portfolio: development of standards for ballistic resistance of personal body armor, bomb disposal robot standards, and computer forensic reference data sets.

January 2007

For additional information contact:
Telephone: (301) 975-2757
Facsimile: (301) 948-0978
On the Web: http://www.eeel.nist.gov/oles/